MW00326021

FROM LIKE TO LOVE

Tim,
Here's to creating
Love!

FROM LIKE
TO
LOVE

Inspiring Emotional Commitment

from Employees and Customers

KEITH ALPER

LIONCREST
PUBLISHING

FROM LIKE TO LOVE

Inspiring Emotional Commitment from Employees and Customers

ISBN   978-1-5445-1117-7 *Hardcover*

978-1-5445-1116-0 *Paperback*

978-1-5445-1115-3 *Ebook*

CONTENTS

ACKNOWLEDGMENTS

This book is a reflection of my work and the work of the team at CPG (cpgagency.com). This job is our passion, and we strive to connect and engage with our teams. We all *love* what we do, we love our clients, and the company we work for. There's nothing like our rock star team at CPG and our Nitrous Effect agencies. Thank you for your commitment to engagement, innovation, and connecting people.

I have many people to thank. I'd like to thank all who contributed to this book. Thank you for sharing your experiences and what you do, your successes and great ideas. Thank you Steve Friedman, Sylvan Schulz, Jennifer Oertli, Sam Paasch, and David Stillman for helping with content, concepts, review, ideas, and feedback on this book.

Lastly, I dedicate this book to the *loves* of my life: my children, Max and Zoe, who are the world to me. And to my late wife, Nancy Alper, who passed away in June of 2017 from breast cancer. We were married for twenty-five years. She was my collaborator in everything I did, from work to ideas, and most importantly, our family. Thank you to our friends and family that provided *love* to us during the illness and passing of Nancy.

INTRODUCTION

Every senior manager has an ideal picture for their business. They want to deliver a quality product or service, have committed customers, and make a profit. They also want their brand to be well-known and have a good reputation. So, how can they please their customers and make this dream happen? The truth is, the best way to achieve this is through happy employees.

We're all familiar with the term *employee engagement*. Employees who are engaged in their work like what they do and where they do it. They provide excellent service to both the customer and the organization that employs them. But it's not enough for employees to simply *like* the company they work for. If you want them to become brand advocates and pass that commitment along to customers, you must move them from like to *love*.

When you think about something you love—like a book, an app, a brand, or a restaurant—how does it make you feel? *Why* do you love it? How do people sound when they express their love for a brand, a company, or the simple pleasures in their lives? They are enthusiastic, and their tone indicates *fulfillment*. They'll say, "I *love* Starbucks," or "I *love* chocolate." This quality of fulfillment is important when moving employees from like to love, because your people are your number one resource, and their happiness affects everything: your product, brand, and bottom line.

INSPIRATION AND MOTIVATION

When employees show up to work, we assume they like their jobs. We don't tend to think there are people who dislike or even hate their jobs. Some might work at a company because the pay is good or their office is close to home, even when they don't particularly like what the organization stands for. Others might feel that management doesn't respect them, but they continue working because they need a paycheck.

It's difficult and a major leap to move an employee from *dislike* to love, so let's consider those who actually like their jobs. What's keeping them from crossing over into "love mode?" What's the missing piece?

To go from like to love, there has to be an aspect of the

job that truly inspires and motivates—it must go beyond compensation. I'm not talking about bringing in Ping-Pong tables for employee leisure time. That may improve morale, but it won't inspire. To motivate employees, you must give them a voice and involve them in something bigger than themselves. There must be an emotional connection and commitment. You have to give them an opportunity to make contributions and be recognized. People want to be *valued* for what they do.

COMMUNICATION IS KEY

Cultural problems often surface in large organizations because employees feel disconnected from the enterprise. In our changing times, people no longer want the same old cookie-cutter communications: blast emails, monthly newsletters, or annual reviews. Social media has set the precedent for instant feedback from family and friends, and people expect the same from their employers—this is especially true for Millennials and Generation Z.

It's therefore vital for companies to shine a spotlight on exceptional people, the ones who go above and beyond in their jobs. Is this something you do on a regular basis? Do you share impactful stories and keep the momentum going? Do you share next steps and what's on the horizon, and involve employees along the way?

While company intranets were useful in their day, they are becoming obsolete. Convenient apps like Slack and Facebook Workplace are quickly replacing them. They provide real-time updates and platforms where employees can interact and stay connected. It doesn't matter if your company is a giant enterprise or a small nonprofit organization—constant, interactive communication is key to a successful transition from like to love.

WINDOWS OF TRANSPARENCY

With the advent of portals and websites like Glassdoor, Yelp, and LinkedIn, every aspect of your company is transparent to the public. Employees are free to post reviews about management and the work environment, and customers don't hesitate to write about bad experiences. Even vendors and suppliers—an overlooked group of people when it comes to company ratings—will post about their business experiences with companies. If they are mistreated by your staff or not paid in a timely manner, they can make it known. Anyone and everyone can give ratings based on a star or number system.

Just as management looks at résumés before interviewing candidates, many potential recruits look at online reviews before choosing an employer. Will they choose to work for a company with a record stained with negative comments from employees, angry customer reviews, and pending lawsuits? Or will they seek out an employer who receives praise for their company culture? Happy customers and happy employees create vast recruiting opportunities through rave reviews. Companies that truly value people and cultivate a culture of love project that transparent image out to the world.

THE COST OF DISENGAGEMENT

Over the past two decades, leading companies have been competing in a "war for talent." Competition is fierce in the hiring and retention of top recruits. However, talented job seekers aren't just looking for higher salaries and better benefits. They're looking for inspiring work environments and company cultures that engage and value employees.

Company loyalty is earned every step of the way. The fact is that companies who don't nurture loyalty and engagement pay the price in disengaged employees who aren't advocates for the brand. Disengagement is a major factor in rapid staff turnover and additional expenses in recruitment and training. It costs far more to onboard and train a new employee than it does to keep one. Engaged employees are company assets who build customer and vendor relationships and brand loyalty. They are representatives of a cultural shift that's moving from like to love.

THE NITROUS EFFECT

In my work as CEO of a seven-agency organization called The Nitrous Effect, I'm on the front lines of complex brand challenges every day. We work with high-profile brands, such as Carnival Cruise Line, Panera, Ulta Beauty, Southwest Airlines, and other brands that are loved both by their customers and employees. Of course, we enjoy working with clients who already have successful corporate cultures and who are always seeking ways to improve. They learn from us and we learn from them too, sharing methods and strategies. We also enjoy the challenge of working with clients who need to revamp their company culture and move employees and customers from like to love.

CPG Agency is our engagement agency, and since we're in the business of helping companies *with* employee engagement, we need to "walk the walk" and live it ourselves. We practice what we preach! We aren't perfect—no company is—but our culture is one of love, and we strive to exceed expectations at every level of engagement. When the FedEx person shows up with deliveries, we thank him or her with Hershey's Kisses. We consider Valentine's Day to be a companywide "national holiday." It's a day we like to make our clients feel extra special, so we send treats and cards with updates just to let them know we care. It's an extension of how we operate every day. We believe company culture should be all-inclusive, with intertwined strategies that recognize and engage customers, employees, and vendors in ways they can feel the love.

An important part of building our company culture is having regular meetings to discuss how we can improve our services as a team, and how we can be more helpful to our clients. We have a strong focus and family-first approach to improve and maintain work-life balance for our employees. It's one of our highest priorities. We offer work-at-home days, flexible locations and hours, and paid days off to volunteer at nonprofit organizations or attend company-sponsored events.

THE HEIGHTS OF SUCCESS

Why is our client, Southwest Airlines, the country's most profitable airline? We know they have low fares, no change fees, and no luggage fees. There's no doubt these features have contributed to their success, but what about the positive customer experience that generates repeat business? It comes from their engaged employees, both union and nonunion.

The overwhelming majority of Southwest Airlines' employees, even those who are union, love working for the company. Southwest fully immerses their teams, listens to staff, communicates clearly, and hosts leadership and employee rallies. I'm often amazed and inspired by what they do to build a culture of engagement, and their business results show they are doing something right. Southwest is a great brand that offers a great product, with a great team, and great results!

FROM LIKE TO LOVE

The gap between like and love is as small as the space between your thumb and pointer finger when you hold them together. Large-change initiatives can bridge that gap, but they aren't always necessary. You don't have to host large rallies like Southwest Airlines to kick up employee engagement. You don't need to hire an outside consultant, invest millions of dollars, or spend hours conducting endless research. Often, small incremental steps are all it takes to create a movement toward a culture of love.

In this book, we'll discuss "like to love" principles that apply to all organizations, large and small. We'll explore how organizations can meet five basic needs to foster employee emotional connection and impact their beliefs and behaviors. I'll present a design process with specific tools you can use to transition your employees from like to love. I'll also share case studies and advice directly from the leaders of companies that have successfully built dynamic cultures of engagement. You'll learn strategies and methods along the way, some of which can be implemented in just *one day*.

Now is the time to do all you can to make sure your employees are fulfilled in their work lives. It's time to create brand advocates and take employee engagement to the next step. It's time to build a culture of all-out, full-employee involvement, and go for the love!

PART ONE

GETTING FROM LIKE TO LOVE

Chapter One

TALENT: THERE'S A WAR GOING ON

A few years ago, we experienced the Great Recession, and it seemed like everyone was out of a job. Contrast that with the state of the economy today, and we see that this is no longer the case—the economy is hot! Recent college graduates have no trouble finding jobs, and employees receive raises left and right. Companies want to hire the best people out there, and they actively recruit in this present-day talent war. However, mere recruitment isn't enough—organizations must put forth the effort to retain employees as well.

Employees who are unhappy or simply *like* your company are a flight risk—it's just a matter of time before they leave. They can easily be "recruited away" and decide to work for another organization. On the other hand, employees who love where they work will find it difficult to leave, even if they could make more money elsewhere.

Millennials and Generation Z are the new workforce, and they only add heat to the talent war. Generation Z includes people between the ages of fourteen and twenty-one, and they are different from the generations that precede them. They have high levels of skill in data, programming, and writing code when they graduate from high school. Since these skills are in high demand, they often have the option to skip college and immediately earn huge salaries with high-tech companies. This is wonderful news for a number of organizations, but members of Generation Z tend to get numerous job offers, and if they don't love your company, it will be nearly impossible to recruit them. Companies need to take action and prepare for the changing needs and expectations of Millennials and Gen Z, while working to inspire and motivate top talent of *all ages*.

A CRISIS OF TALENT

According to a 2014 report from Deloitte Global Human Capital Trends Research, 79 percent of business leaders believe they have a significant employee engagement problem.[1] Many leaders we work with today are con-

---

1   Bersin, Josh; Flynn, Jason; Mazor, Art; Melian, Veronica, "The employee experience: Culture, engagement, and beyond," Deloitte Insights, Feb. 28, 2017, https://www2.deloitte.com/insights/us/en/focus/human-capital-trends/2017/improving-the-employee-experience-culture-engagement.html.

cerned—even worried—about hiring top talent and keeping them engaged. In our business, we've become painfully aware that some people absolutely *hate* their jobs. Others don't trust management, and they are fed up with their company saying one thing and doing another. According to Gallup research, after a year on the job, 70 percent of people are no longer engaged at work, and this lack of engagement costs companies up to $550 billion per year in lost productivity.[2] These statistics only heighten today's crisis of talent.

WHO COMES FIRST?

The experience at the Walgreens near my house is unlike any other. A woman who works there runs throughout the store to help customers, sings into the PA system, and joyfully does her job. I believe she might be the world's best employee.

Her happiness makes her a wonderful brand advocate—she's obviously committed to the organization and its goals. Customers feel good about the store and want to return. Coworkers enjoy their work environment because her happiness is contagious. Her attitude provides smarter outcomes, and she is moving the business forward.

---

2   Gallup 2017 State of the American Workplace Report, https://news.gallup.com/reports/199961/state-american-workplace-report-2017.aspx.

It's awesome to see such an engaged employee, but this brings us to the billion-dollar question: who is your first priority to make happy—employees or customers?

Some company leaders believe employees should be the priority, and others believe it should be the customers. The fact is, if you put employees first, they will take care of the customers.

Execution of strategies will differ from company to company, but the employee-customer relationship is symbiotic—it's interrelated, no matter the company. Happy employees who love what they do serve customers well, and do whatever it takes to help the company's bottom line. They're more willing to stay late and go above and beyond in their daily responsibilities. Engaged employees are priceless. They are the key to customer satisfaction.

THE COST OF TURNOVER

Engaged employees are invaluable, but unhappy employees end up costing an organization money. Disengaged employees aren't loyal to their company, and when a workforce is disengaged, it results in rapid turnover. Every industry is different, but it's costly to recruit someone new, and turnover is even more expensive.

For example, we work with a health system that has a high

rate of turnover, and it costs them about $55,000 to recruit and train a new nurse. We understand there are circumstances that cause employees to leave, such as relocation, but we know of *several* hospital systems that are understaffed by thousands of people! Employees are leaving in droves, and this doesn't just cost hospitals a fortune—it creates a massive shortage of talented, much-needed staff.

Why are so many hospital employees leaving their jobs? It's possible the organizations are doing a poor job of communicating, aren't listening to employee feedback, or aren't recognizing employee contributions. Or it could be due to changes in the economy, which have opened up new gigs via home health opportunities, neighborhood urgent care clinics, nursing homes, and more. The talent wars, a wealth of new options, and the increasing demand for an engaging company culture can be a formula for success, or disaster.

When employees love where they work, they provide smarter outcomes, and they'll stick with an organization for the long term. They become brand advocates who actively move the business forward. This is a no-brainer: get your employees engaged!

CASE STUDY: TESLA VERSUS FORD

You're probably familiar with the car company Tesla, the

hard-driving startup that burst onto the scene a few years ago. They're industry innovators and changers, and even though they have a demanding CEO, people love working there. Why? Because they feel like they're part of something that matters; they build something significant every day. The company demands hard work and expects everyone to go above and beyond, but it's worth it to the employees because they're on the cutting edge and reap the financial rewards.

Ford, on the other hand, is behind the curve when it comes to manufacturing electric vehicles, and employee engagement is lacking. There's not much love. Ford struggled during the economic downturn, and they're still long overdue in the release of certain product lines. Recently, Ford's board of directors fired its CEO because they realized they lagged so far behind Tesla. And now, Ford has reduced production of most of its car line.

What it comes down to is this: if you can move your employees from like to love, you will win the talent war.

END OF CHAPTER CHECKLIST/CHEAT SHEET

- Do your employees love working for you? How do you measure this love?

- Who comes first at your company—employees or customers?

- Does your company have a crisis of talent?

- Do you know the cost of turnover at your company?

- Are you making changes to create and provide a more loving environment?

- If you were to write a case study of your own company, how would you describe the level of employee satisfaction?

Chapter Two

FORGET EMPLOYEE ENGAGEMENT: GO FOR THE LOVE!

Why is Google thriving and Yahoo has all but disappeared? Quality products and services play a part in the success of an organization, but I believe it all starts and ends with company culture. When someone has a solid career and can choose between competing workplaces in the same industry, culture is the main differentiator.

CREATING A "LOVEABLE" CULTURE

A loveable corporate culture begins at the top of the organization, with senior leadership setting the tone. Their priorities are made obvious to employees through their everyday actions, and those become the spirit of the culture. For example, if they only care about financial results, that will be the sole motivation behind everyone's daily tasks. While good financial results benefit employees, shareholders, and stakeholders, top companies make establishing a positive company culture their top priority. A business that is all about profits will never succeed.

Corporate culture can't be an "also-ran." The C-suite has to encourage employee love. I understand the word *love* can be hard to embrace, but it truly is the catalyst to success. Have you thought about how your company has accommodated employee needs and requests over the past ten years? Do you know how your salaries rank versus the competition?

An engaging culture requires executive sponsorship, and will positively impact your bottom line if it gets the attention it deserves. When leaders put their people first and focus to make sure employees love the company, it pays off. They get happy, engaged employees and the natural sequence of success that follows.

EMOTIONAL BANK ACCOUNT

Think of company culture as an emotional bank account. You constantly put in deposits, and you have the option to make withdrawals. For example, if your company plans to institute a policy that some employees don't like, you must have enough in your emotional bank account to make a withdrawal.

If the account is well-padded, the unfavorable policy won't create an overdraft. Every company makes mistakes, but if you always put culture and engagement first, the emotional bank account will be full.

I know we've made mistakes at our company. We do all we can to put our employees first, but occasionally, something that aligns with company goals doesn't align with what employees want.

For example, our company was small when it first began, and there weren't many women in the organization. After our workforce grew and became more diverse, it was brought to our attention that we needed to make changes to our maternity-leave policy. As male leaders, we weren't aware of the ways in which it was lacking until two female employees approached us with proposed changes. New mothers needed more time off and the option to work from home or bring their babies into the office. We reviewed their requests and updated the policy immediately. This was a small change, but it made a big difference; it was easy, and it was the right thing to do. We went from having no plan at all to creating a robust one, which helped move our employees from like to love.

PULSE CHECK

A doctor checks your pulse when you go in for a physical because it's a vitally important indicator of how your entire body is functioning. In the same fashion, it's imperative to check the pulse of your organization. Every company has good and bad days—they even have good and bad months. Pulse checks keep leadership informed of these less-than-ideal days, and they can use the information gathered to find solutions.

There are many ways to conduct pulse checks, but they have to be *real*. You must execute them in an effective manner, understand the results, and plan to address the areas that may need attention. To get you brainstorming, I'll share a pulse check method we use at our agency, CPG.

We have a meter with red and green buttons near our exit that asks employees, "How was your day today?" They can choose green or red before they go home for the day, and the data then goes to our chief operating officer (COO).

We don't fret too much if there are a couple of reds. We know it could be because employees have stressful events in their personal lives, or they may have had some difficulty with a coworker that morning, or perhaps they're dealing with a demanding client situation or project. When the majority of employees choose red, however, we know it's time to investigate.

When this happens, leadership huddles together and asks, "What's going on?" Then we do employee surveys to dig deep. We ask staff to rank many different areas, such as work environment, tools and resources, work quality, and overall satisfaction. We also ask them to share their thoughts on our strategic partnerships when appropriate. We're transparent about the results: we share the good, the bad, and the ugly. We don't BS our employees. We explain what's happening and we work collectively to come up with solutions.

Recording and investigating "red days" is part of the continual care and feeding of our corporate culture—we view them as opportunities to examine how we can improve and make changes where necessary to show employees the love.

TRANSPARENCY IS CRITICAL

Transparency is also critical in creating a culture of love. What has become apparent from the stories that have emerged from the "Me Too" movement is that there is a lack of transparency at many companies. The truth is often hidden behind lawsuits and secret payouts.

In today's digital age, it's impossible for companies to hide their true colors. Employees expect honesty from their employers—they expect not to be lied to. This is especially true for Millennials—who are 50 percent of the current workforce—because they are accustomed to unlimited access to information. They are far less tolerant of secrets than previous generations, and we've seen that open communication is more prevalent in younger companies than in older ones. Millennials want to know what a company is doing, why they are doing it, and they want to know *immediately*—they demand transparency. Companies can no longer hide information under the carpet or try to blend it into gray areas.

Of course, issues around transparency don't always involve full-blown scandals. More common are employee concerns about promotions, raises, and bonuses. Companies should be honest with their employees. Important company-related news needs to be shared. It doesn't matter if it's good or bad. Being open with your people lets them know you're all in this together.

Sharing bad news with my employees isn't fun, but I don't put it off—I share it truthfully, and I share it immediately. We share disappointment in losses, but I get to deliver good news, too, and then we celebrate wins. We share *everything*.

THE TOP TWENTY-FIVE

With the heat turned up in the talent war, companies are eager to appear in the top twenty-five on "Best Places to

Work" lists. These are regularly featured in *Forbes*, *Fortune*, *USA Today*, and in local or regional publications. However, companies don't realize that it takes work to get on—and stay on—those lists.

Recently, we worked with an organization that wanted to be on a "Best Places to Work" list right away. However, the change that was necessary for them to achieve that goal wasn't going to happen overnight. They needed to refine their culture, infuse a healthier work environment, and establish clear lines of communication. These elements of change weren't unique to them—they would have been necessary for most organizations to make it to the top twenty-five of "Best Places to Work."

We explained that even after the changes are implemented, it will take time to see the results. It could be a year or two before employees begin saying, "This company is wonderful. I'm engaged, and they have a diverse, inclusive community. Leadership listens to me and communicates well. I'm proud to work here!"

The series of steps required to make the list might sound simple, but the reality is, it's difficult to get on, and even harder to stay. Once a company makes it into the top twenty-five, their status is not secured. A giant one-time initiative isn't enough to hold their position, and organizations strive to remain on the list year after year.

SENDING MIXED MESSAGES

Basic information must be communicated to employees in a direct and consistent manner. Be clear about their job responsibilities and whom they report to, and provide direction on how they can succeed with the company. Sending mixed messages about authority and responsibility won't create a culture of love—leaders can't say one thing and then do another.

A retail client's company executive told us, "We want our managers to feel like they own the store." However, when we toured their stores and talked to their managers, they said, "Not only do we *not* feel like we own the store, we don't even feel like we have a say in everyday matters."

We had to identify the source of disconnect and get everyone in the organization on the same page. Since the managers didn't feel like they owned the store, senior leadership took time to listen to their concerns and found ways to give them more autonomy. Managers were given the authority to: hire new staff; determine compensation, bonuses, and promotions; and select merchandise for their location. As the transition occurred and managers were given more decision-making freedom, it was no surprise that sales and employee satisfaction increased as a result.

CASE STUDY: SOUTHWEST AIRLINES

It may not be a coincidence that Southwest Airlines is based out of Love Field in Dallas, Texas. Their logo is love, and they are the perfect example of a company that has successfully transitioned employees from like to love. Even if they weren't a client, they would still be my favorite airline—I believe they are the North Star for how a company should be run.

According to Cheryl Hughey, the company's managing director of culture:

> We're a forty-seven-year-old company, and our tactics to create an "employee-first" focus have evolved. Our culture is an essential part of Southwest, and an area of the business we proactively work to preserve. There isn't an exact formula to our unique culture, because culture means something different to everyone, and we want to empower employees to be authentic. We're free to display culture in the way that makes the most sense to us as individuals.

> We're also committed to listening to employees' feedback and tuning into their sentiment. Knowing how employees feel day-to-day in their work environment helps move the needle from, "I like my job," to "I love my job." Our leaders strive for positive daily leader/employee interaction, where employees feel heard, respected, and informed.

Many Southwest Airlines employees are union workers, which means they have intermediary representation between themselves and the organization. While the company and the unions may disagree from time to time, Southwest maintains strong relationships with the union groups. In fact, union employees are some of the company's biggest advocates. Their love for Southwest speaks volumes about their company culture.

To their credit, Southwest Airlines has turned hiring into an art form. They know employees are more likely to be engaged if they get the right people into the right roles, so they take hiring very seriously—they almost act like movie producers casting for roles. Finding the best fit for each person can make all the difference in the world and creates a solid foundation for employee engagement. The company also offers leading benefits such as a 401(k) matching program and profit sharing to recruit quality employees.

Southwest Airlines is serious about what they do, but they don't take themselves too seriously. On Halloween, even the CEO dresses in a costume, and locations throughout Southwest's vast network are encouraged to demonstrate their fun-loving attitude in various ways. Some might find dressing up to be silly, but it's one example of how the company encourages a fun environment. If employees have fun and enjoy being at work, that feeling gets transferred to the customers.

CASE STUDY: VIRGIN HOTELS

Virgin Hotels is a new company with just one hotel open and a few more being developed around the world. Right now, this is working to their advantage. Richard Branson started the business knowing they had to set themselves apart from the competition. "We want our hotel to be unique," says Branson. "We want it to operate differently than any other. We want to bring in extraordinary people, so they will do extraordinary things."

One thing to love about Virgin Hotels is that they put employees first. They are committed to engagement and transparency within their company, they take care of employees, and they provide an outstanding benefits package. Their employees love working there!

According to Clio Knowles, VP of people:

> We have a Rally at least once per day to get everyone amped up for their shift, and a different manager leads every time. A Rally covers company news, employee birthdays, and a fun culture fact or quote of the day. Recently, we've started asking questions like, "If you could be wealthy now, or live to be one hundred, which would you choose?" Or, sometimes we'll just go completely off script and do a line dance.
>
> We have different events on a weekly or monthly basis, and some aren't planned in advance on a calendar. Today, my

Director of People and I were trying to decide if we could all do a karaoke contest through the Dub Smash app before the end of the year, but since we're already having a holiday party and making gingerbread houses this week, we decided to hold off on the karaoke. We make sure our teammates have fun on the job, while still getting their work done.

The moment you walk into one of their hotels, you can tell this company is different. Employees trade off job responsibilities, which provides a refreshing customer experience. For example, if a bellhop isn't available to get your luggage to your room, another employee will show up at the front desk and assume the role. The company has eliminated silos, so all employees can focus on customer service.

Companies like Virgin Hotels and Southwest Airlines make it their business to deepen employee engagement, and this creates a culture of real heart and caring. They are truly two of the best places to work.

END OF CHAPTER CHECKLIST/CHEAT SHEET

- Do your leaders put their people first and work to ensure that employees love the company?

- Have you thought about how your company accommodates employee needs and requests?

- Do you know how your salaries and benefits rank versus the competition?

- Do you regularly check the "pulse" of your organization?

- Is your company transparent and openly communicative with your employees?

- Is your C-suite committed to a company culture of love?

- What intentional programs have you initiated to build toward that goal?

- What is getting in your way of building a culture that inspires employees?

Chapter Three

CUSTOMER COMMITMENT CAN'T BE COMMODIFIED

Southwest Airlines flies the exact same planes as other airlines, but the customer experience with Southwest is truly unique. I don't want to throw other airlines "under the bus," but if you randomly surveyed one hundred people, I'd bet ninety-five of them would rank their experience with Southwest as the best. The airline is fun and prompt, with friendly pilots, flight attendants, and gate agents. They understand the importance of the customer experience and how it ties into the success of the brand.

Great customer service can only be provided by employees *who love what they do*. It's the only way to build a successful brand that inspires both employees and customers. Earlier, I mentioned the woman who works at the Walgreens near my house. She's been there for twenty years, and I've never seen a happier, nicer, more engaged, unbelievable frontline employee. She should win the customer service Academy Award! She absolutely loves what she does. I often use her as a prime example of an engaged employee because her upbeat attitude becomes associated with the brand.

Think of how your employees approach their work on a less-than-perfect day. Do they roll with the punches and step up? Or do they allow frustration to affect the way they treat customers and coworkers? If employees are engaged, external factors like system malfunctions or inevitable delays won't affect their attitudes.

Many companies are adding a chief experience officer, who is responsible for brand interaction, to their C-suite. Others are adapting the role of their chief marketing officer to include more supervision and administration of the brand experience. These officers may oversee everything that could possibly influence the customer, such as website functionality, appearance of the stores, and employee competency.

The customer experience can't be overlooked, and neither can the experience of employees. As we've already seen, they are interrelated. More than ever, business today is about relationships. Of course, companies sell products—goods and services, which are commodities in the marketplace—but relationships aren't commodities. They can't be bought and sold. They are nurtured through caring.

Let's use Target as a positive example of the customer experience. What's it like when you visit their website? How does it look when you walk into one of their stores? How do you feel about their merchandise? Target has been successful because their stores are clean and well organized, they have exclusive brands and products, and their employees are friendly and knowledgeable—they further enhance the positive aspects of the store and the customer experience.

"Brands" are ultimately defined by their relationships with customers, and between customers and the employees who represent and define them. Companies that strive for customer commitment to their brand will achieve it only through commitment to their employees. They are the face of the brand.

BECOMING BRAND ADVOCATES

The ability to innovate and be creative on the job is an important factor today, especially in the tech industry. Not long ago, Microsoft was written off as an old, stodgy software company, and people considered Apple to be the leader in the industry. However, over the past few years, Microsoft's leadership has created an innovative environment and reenergized the company. Now, they are developing amazing products and services, and are a strong competitor in their industry.

While producing unique and advanced products can work wonders for building brand recognition, much more is needed to turn your employees into *brand advocates*. There must be other compelling reasons for them to joyfully promote your company and its products. Flexible work hours, generous benefits, and on-site amenities definitely help, but there are other, more important aspects that are commonly overlooked.

LEARNING OPPORTUNITIES

Learning opportunities are essential if you want to create brand advocates. Employees need ongoing training and development, and some companies invest quite a bit of money into this aspect of employee development. For example, LinkedIn recently purchased a learning company so they can provide new opportunities to employees. *All* of our Nitrous Effect staff have access to learning programs on a regular basis. This gives them the opportunity to learn about the latest technology, customer service skills, and how to handle critical issues like sexual harassment.

Engaged employees want to better themselves for the

good of the organization, but also for their own futures. We gladly send our employees to continuing education seminars, classes, and meetings. The knowledge and skills they gain ultimately benefit the company, but we also know that learning is necessary so they can progress in their careers.

ADVANCEMENT

Along with providing learning and development opportunities, employees need to know there are opportunities for advancement. Even the happiest of employees will think, "What's my goal for working at this company? Is there a path for advancement? Will I be able to make more money one day? How can I learn more about leadership roles?" Company leaders need to be prepared to answer those questions and explain advancement opportunities. And keep in mind that not everyone wants to become a manager, so it's important to have more than one path.

The Nitrous Effect comprises seven different agencies, so we encourage employees who are seeking new careers to look at internal opportunities before looking elsewhere. If they're unhappy as a member of the video business team, they can look at our digital agency or another area. We enjoy giving people the opportunity to change careers or advance within our organization. Not only does this keep our employees happy and engaged, it increases our retention and keeps recruiting and training costs low.

Companies often run on bright shiny objects, and many have a stubborn streak. They must realize that what has worked in the past may not work today, and they can't do things the way they've always done them. If they continue on this path, they won't survive—they won't retain staff, and they won't keep their customers. There has been a large disruption over the past ten years in technology and communication, so companies *have to change*. Some companies don't catch on to this, and maybe they never will, but no one can stand completely still and be successful. It's also important to note that making changes overnight based on fads is not sustainable. Companies have to keep up with technology and industry trends to grow their business and continually develop their employees.

CASE STUDY: ULTA BEAUTY

Ulta Beauty is one of the fastest-growing beauty retailers in America. They are champions when it comes to turning employees into brand advocates. CPG annually produces a large-scale event for them, with thousands of store managers and field leadership in attendance. This is a weeklong conference where they learn more about the industry, beauty products, hair and skin care, and how to excel in customer service. All of this information is presented in awe-inspiring ways: in general and breakout sessions, trade shows, and learning seminars. This is Ulta's time for employee development, fun, and camaraderie.

The company invests their full energy into this annual event, and the payoff is massive in the form of employee engagement. This supports the concept that training and advancement, along with a healthy, empowering environment, creates brand advocates.

According to Raquel Frankenreider, Senior Vice President, Store Operations:

> One of our values is "Own and love what you do." We want employees to feel great about themselves and their contributions. When their ideas become reality, they've truly been empowered—they reflect and understand the brand.

> We keep our guests and associates at the center of everything we do. We're in the beauty business, and we make people feel good. If they walk in with a problem, we have a solution. Or, if they walk in and want to have fun, we create it for them. We do that for our associates, too, from training to trying new products.

> We create an environment where our associates are empowered to make every guest who walks through the door feel beautiful. And when the guest walks out, the associate is

confident she has made their day. This makes them much more than employees—they are brand ambassadors.

Ulta's CEO, Mary Dillon, is a rock star, along with every member of the leadership team. Through their transparency and education, they're absolutely killing it with employees. When CPG first had the opportunity to place a bid with them, I asked my wife if she had ever heard of the company.

"Yes!" she replied. "I'm there almost every day. I go there for anything from three-dollar lip gloss to a twenty-dollar shampoo."

After learning she was a loyal Ulta Beauty customer, we decided to visit a store together. It didn't take long before I realized it was the real deal. They had a brow bar to get your eyebrows done, an in-store hair salon, and various product specials. You could find anything and everything at that one location alone, and the employees were extremely knowledgeable.

CASE STUDY: L. KEELEY CONSTRUCTION

L. Keeley Construction is a mid-sized construction company that owns several businesses. They provide learning opportunities every month for each of their companies through a program called KeeleyU. This is a serious investment in their employee development, and they allow employees to take time out of their workday for learning. Development and advancement is a big deal for them, and the investment pays off through knowledgeable, empowered employees and the confidence to promote from within the organization.

According to Rusty Keeley, CEO:

> We consider everyone at Keeley family, which is why we don't call our people employees; we call them "Keeley'ns." To take that a step further, we've developed a culture based on four core principles: fun, family, accountability, and results. As a family, we want to make sure every member has the resources needed to succeed. We have a concept called "fail forward" to encourage everyone to continually better themselves. We don't fear pushing Keeley'ns out of their comfort zones to help them reach their full potential. This has created a family culture, and our people feel valued and empowered.

> The family aspect is important to us, but we also emphasize a culture of personal and professional development through KeeleyU courses. Team members have access to world-class speakers to learn and help advance their careers. The courses are facilitated on company time and encompass a wide range of subjects.

We want to create a culture worth sharing, and for people to be proud of what our company stands for. We have a strong social media presence across multiple channels, and we use that to encourage team members to share their feelings about our culture. This has turned everyone into a brand ambassador, and they are a catalyst for the recruitment of more Keeley'ns. We also have an internal newsletter to share what's happening at each location, and to keep team members up to date on their fellow Keeley'ns.

L. Keeley Construction provides better service than their competitors because they don't just study the construction industry—they examine trends to determine what the future holds. This allows them to find the best ways to build, approach new systems, and deliver to customers. The establishment of KeeleyU as an employee resource takes development a step further by empowering and educating their staff.

CASE STUDY: SOUTHWEST AIRLINES

Southwest Airlines builds its business on its people. Through open communication and creating an environment of trust, they turn employees into brand advocates.

According to Cheryl Hughey, the company's managing director of culture:

We believe the most important factor in creating brand advocates is trust. When employees trust what leaders are sharing, we create an environment where employees feel informed, understand the direction of the company and any changes that are taking place, and how we'll work through those changes to get to our end goal. This openness also helps employees see how their roles fit into the big picture. It gives them confidence in the company, and they take pride in how they are contributing to Southwest. Being a member of our winning team is not only fun—it triggers a feeling that makes everyone want to *continue* building it. I know that when our employees are associated with Southwest, even if it's wearing a branded shirt on their personal time, it's something they take pride in.

CASE STUDY: VIRGIN HOTELS

Virgin Hotels's leadership believes the key to creating brand advocates is authenticity and remaining true to your word.

According to Clio Knowles, VP of people:

To create brand advocates, you have to be authentic. People see right through you if you're not being yourself—you must be transparent and genuine. We've created a brand based on our philosophy, and we have to live up to that. I can't tell people it's all about love, and then yell at them to "whip them into shape." I have to live the philosophy every day at work. When I visited our hotel in Chicago a few weeks ago, I promised to follow up with some employees after we had a discussion, and I did. If you aren't being authentic, they will know.

CASE STUDY: SEARS

After football games, teams can watch "game films" to see what they did right, and what they did wrong—they want to see how and if they can do things better next time. Unfortunately, not every case study featured in this book is a success story, and if we were to watch the game film of Sears, we'd see financial and management plays that didn't work.

Believe it or not, Sears was once in the S&P 500. In fact, they were a top 100 company. They invented the catalog and direct order, and consumers considered them to be the darling of retail stores for many years. However, the company was never open to change.

In a hedge fund financial play, they were bought out several years ago. This transaction took place without giving any thought to how it would affect employees and customers. If you visit one of their stores today, you can see the results of their poor decisions: their merchandise is lacking and they have uninspired employees. Can you remember the last time you walked into a Sears to make a purchase? I can't.

Imagine how dreadful it would be to work at Sears right now. There's no high-quality merchandise, fewer vendors are shipping, and the store is empty. It's sad, considering they were once America's top retailer. Sears could have had a different outcome had they been an employee-first organization. Employees want to innovate and be inspired. They don't want to be in defensive mode at all times and wonder if the company is going under.

Organizations must realize change and innovation are necessary. This is true for all areas of the business: markets, meeting customer needs, and creating employee engagement. Sears is an example of what can happen when an organization fails to make the appropriate investments in their stores and in their employees.

END OF CHAPTER CHECKLIST/CHEAT SHEET

- Do your employees love what they do?

- Does your company have a chief experience officer? Who's watching the brand experience?

- Are your employees brand advocates?

- Do you provide learning opportunities and educational development for your staff?

- Do your employees have opportunities to grow and advance their careers within the company?

Chapter Four

THE FIVE BASIC NEEDS: YOU'D BETTER MEET THEM

If you want to bridge the gap from like to love, you have to build emotional connections that impact employee beliefs and behavior. One way to do this is to facilitate work-life integration.

Rather than use the term *work-life balance*, we refer to this concept as *work-life integration*. Companies used to expect employees to address personal matters on their own time, but that's no longer realistic. If you are supposed to be working at 10:00 a.m., but you need to take your child to a doctor's appointment at that time, making the appointment isn't about balance. It's about integration, because the two events are intertwined. With current advances in technology and connectivity, it's no longer necessary to work strict nine-to-five days, and it's not uncommon for employees to respond to work texts and emails at 11:00 p.m.

THE FIVE BASIC NEEDS

Work-life integration is just one way your company can meet the five basic needs. These needs don't just apply to employees and the workplace—they are the key to building lasting, meaningful relationships in life, so you'd better meet all of them! So, what are the five basic needs?

1. You genuinely care about me.
2. I trust you and you trust me.
3. You listen to me.
4. You appreciate me for who I am and you tell me so.
5. We share a meaningful purpose.

If you only take away one thing from this book, it should be these five basic needs—they are the ingredients of The Nitrous Effect's "love potion." Let's take a closer look at these five basic needs and creative, simple ways you can meet them.

1. YOU GENUINELY CARE ABOUT ME

Today, personal and professional lives overlap more

than ever. As a result, employees expect empathy from their employers and accommodations for their personal lives. This could mean they have the option of working from home, their company offers meditation classes for stress relief, or they have access to an on-site health and wellness program. My company purposely moved into a building with a gym, swimming pool, and locker room because to us, providing employees with the opportunity to take care of themselves while they are at work is a priority. We want to show them that we genuinely care about them.

2. I TRUST YOU AND YOU TRUST ME

You've probably heard the quote, "People don't leave companies, they leave managers." A job is defined by the people you work with and managers have to build trust. Oftentimes, a person's boss is the one authority figure they interact with on a regular basis, and to them, they represent the entire organization. Statistics even show that employee happiness falls upon their direct supervisor.[3] How's that for putting on the pressure?

Maybe you worked for a wonderful company in the past, but your manager was a complete ass. He or she didn't

---

3 Leah Fessler, "A New Study Shows How Managers Can Double Employee Satisfaction and Trust," Quartz at Work, October 30, 2017, https://work.qz.com/1108444/employee-satisfaction-and-trust-is-tightly-linked-to-manager-support/.

give you credit for anything, didn't answer questions, and played favorites. You didn't trust this person, and you didn't feel safe. This is the type of scenario that must be avoided at all costs. If an employee doesn't trust their boss or the organization, I guarantee they'll soon be gone.

The Best Resignation

Recently, a Nitrous Effect employee resigned because he wanted to pursue a new career path. Losing talented individuals is always a disappointment, but this time it was slightly different for us.

This employee had challenges when he first joined our organization. He often struggled, and even though I didn't have all the answers, I did my best to help him. To use the title of Kim Scott's best-selling book *Radical Candor*, that's exactly what I used: radical candor. When he left our company three years later, he sent an email thanking me for steering him in the right direction. He wrote, "I would not have been able to make my next career move without your help. I give you one hundred percent credit for helping me. I love your company, I love you guys, and I appreciate all you've done." He sent this message despite the rocky road we had experienced, and it was an affirmation that we had handled his situation the right way.

3. YOU LISTEN TO ME

People are reluctant to stay at companies where the important decisions are made on the fifteenth floor. Employees must feel they have a voice if they are going to commit to their work and to an organization. Channels of communication must be easily accessible so employees can express ideas, opinions, concerns, and participate in decision-making. It doesn't matter if you're a three-person operation or a multibillion-dollar company—it's imperative to give employees a voice in your organization. *Everyone* wants to be heard.

Realistically, not every employee can make decisions for a company, but all of them want to feel valued—there must be a legitimate way for them to share their thoughts and feelings. This can be as easy as conducting group polls or allowing teams to collaborate on new ideas.

At our Nitrous Effect agencies, everyone is welcome to present ideas to leaders—our doors are always open. We welcome radical candor and confrontation, and our employees know they won't get fired for expressing their opinions, as long as they are respectful and refrain from personal attacks. Employees can come to us and say something like, "Hey, we're understaffed, and it's killing us. Please do something about it."

We also ask for employee input when it comes to problem-solving and gathering new ideas. "Hey, everyone. We see an issue looming on the horizon, and we've come up with three possible solutions. Which do you think is best?" Or, if we're developing new software or considering a new company policy, we ask for input.

There are several ways we ask for employees to contribute their thoughts and ideas. We may crowdsource or do an email blast and ask for a response within thirty minutes. Or we might hold an open forum or an idea-pitching session if we need to work quickly. We've found that when everyone participates in the process, we have their buy-in and support. We'll discuss these survey methods in detail later in the book.

4. YOU APPRECIATE ME FOR WHO I AM AND YOU TELL ME SO

The desire to be recognized and appreciated is universal. Showing employees appreciation and acknowledging their efforts in the workplace are essential to the end goal of building a culture of love.

Companies like Southwest Airlines and Ulta Beauty that regularly recognize their employees are winning. Have you thought about how your organization recognizes people with unique perspectives and skills? How are their contributions being acknowledged? When we get an unsolicited email from a client singing an employee's praises, we give that person a special cash bonus. It's one of several ways we show appreciation and recognition, and it motivates everyone to continue delivering excellent customer service.

Recognition serves the dual purpose of motivating and building community, and it has to be *real*. When employee efforts are acknowledged in front of upper-level management and their peers, their level of commitment goes through the roof. They will go all in and love your company once they know they are truly appreciated for their individual contributions.

5. WE SHARE A MEANINGFUL PURPOSE

Gallup research reveals that a clear mission and purpose is a huge source of motivation.[4] Employees want to know the organization's mission and values, and whether or not they share the same ones, so you must build and communicate your mission into everyone's daily work. You must repeat it, reinforce it, live it, and make clear how individual roles contribute to it. One way we do this is by having a Core Values wall on display in the office.

The Nitrous Effect values collaboration, integrity, and respect. We clearly communicate those values, and we

---

4   Gallup 2017 State of the American Workplace Report, https://news.gallup.com/reports/199961/state-american-workplace-report-2017.aspx.

demonstrate them to our employees and customers every day. If our organization does or says something that contradicts our values, employees can call us, or one another, on it. We encourage employees to set up meetings with leadership to discuss issues, but just because someone calls another person out, it doesn't mean the other party has to agree with them.

Openly communicating our core values and expectations benefits the company and strongly contributes to employee engagement. However, it can create uncomfortable situations from time to time. For instance, we've had to part ways with talented people in our organization due to a consistent lack of respect for others, and we've rejected business from potential clients who've asked us to participate in unethical practices. As unpleasant as this can be, occasional discomfort is a small price to pay to demonstrate to our people that we share a meaningful purpose.

As part of our shared purpose, we regularly help people in our community who are in need. We work alongside many nonprofit organizations, and we regularly raise and donate money to a cancer research hospital. Last year, people in our company spent four hours making 10,000 meals for the homeless. We brought in an outside agency for help, shut down operations for the day, and everyone participated, including freelancers. It was an excellent team- and culture-building experience—we were more than happy to invest money for this project. Our employees have already told us they'd like to do more activities like this one, because it gave them the opportunity to be a part of something bigger than themselves. They felt they were making a difference.

Another mission at The Nitrous Effect is that we want to show everyone the love, and we mean *everyone*—not just employees and customers. For instance, we take special care of UPS delivery drivers, vendors, and visitors, just to name a few.

It doesn't matter who visits our office—we want to "wow" them. We welcome them into our office the same way we would welcome them into our homes, and then some. At CPG, we create an extra-special experience for visitors, clients, and guests. We turn on spotlights, and always have food and snacks available to make it social and fun. We put up a marquee that displays the visitor's name, and we give them VIP parking. We want them to have the ultimate brand experience at our agencies and leave our offices knowing we truly care about them.

END OF CHAPTER CHECKLIST/CHEAT SHEET

- In what ways are you building emotional connections that impact employee beliefs and behaviors?

- Are you committed to the five ingredients of the "love potion?"

- Are you building a company culture of genuine caring, mutual trust, open communication, appreciation, and meaningful purpose?

- How do you recognize a team member who has been named by a client for outstanding work or service?

Chapter Five

A STREAMLINED APPROACH: LITTLE THINGS MEAN A LOT

The transition from like to love will be different for every company. It depends on the size and existing culture of each individual department and the organization as a whole. There's no one-size-fits-all solution—each company is as unique as the people who work for them, and several factors must be considered before creating and implementing a plan.

Startups and newer companies will have a different strategy than older, more established ones, and large companies may have different issues than small businesses. One company may only need to make some minor tweaks to encourage the transition, while another may have a higher hill to climb. However, no matter your company's current situation, making the change might be easier than you think.

We've tried many different approaches at The Nitrous Effect, and we've discovered that a simple adjustment like changing the dress code or work hours can be extremely impactful. I'll share some of the things we've done and provide some fresh ideas to help you begin thinking outside of the box.

GIVE IT A TRY

We take the pulse of our employees through surveys to find out what makes them tick, and most of the time, it's not just money. They want other things, like greater comfort at work or the ability to express themselves more freely. They want to learn, be heard, be inspired, and be part of the solution. "Top-down" hasn't worked for a long time, and sometimes all it takes is a little tweak to move from like to love.

For example, many CPG clients are Fortune 500 companies, so we used to be business casual with blue-jean Fridays to sync up with them, but our team didn't want a rigid dress code. When we moved into a new building a few years ago, the offices were dusty and unfinished. We decided to allow everyone to wear jeans whenever they wanted, so they wouldn't ruin any nice clothes. A few years have passed, and we never returned to the business casual dress code—our people come to work wearing everyday casual. Of course, there are exceptions, like when a client plans to visit; we notify everyone in advance to dress up on a certain date. As minor as the dress code change was, it had a huge impact on how people felt about working for us, and it moved them farther along the path from like to love.

We've also experimented with changing up the work hours, especially in the summer. Changes like this don't require a lot of money, effort, or a majority vote from the board of directors. They do, however, require an open mind and discernment about what is important, and will have the greatest impact for your people.

TIME FOR FUN

We can't afford to offer certain amenities like a fully paid cafeteria or on-site laundry service, so we try to find other perks that allow employees to let their hair down and have a little fun. We started a tradition called "Beer Cart Friday." I understand this may not be a suitable option for a bank or an insurance company, but in our creative and stressful industry, it works, and it's low cost. It's just something we offer for fun, and employees aren't required to drink a beer to participate.

We also look for opportunities for fun outside of Beer Cart Friday—we try to turn everything into a special occasion. On March 14 at 3:14, we stop working, bring in various pies, and celebrate "Pi Day." Our employees love it! We also bring in fresh fruit every week, and we give away free tickets to the events we produce. Sadly, many organizations dismiss the thought of having fun at work—they don't realize how easy and affordable it can be to infuse a little joy into their culture.

ENGAGEMENT COUNCILS

We've helped many clients create what we call an *engagement council*. It's a group that is connected to human resources, but operates outside of it and represents many levels of the company. These councils are beneficial because they allow you to take the pulse of your organization at various intervals—annually, monthly, weekly, or even daily. The council is informed of issues within the company and works to resolve them. They also have the opportunity to be proactive and find out employee likes and dislikes, and what drives motivation—their goal is to make a positive impact and facilitate employee engagement.

Council members can be employees and/or senior leadership, outside consultants, or a combination of the three groups. There are many ways to form an employee engagement council, but the desired end result is moving employees from like to love. We've found that these councils work best when they are self-led, meaning within the organization or individual departments. This is because it's easy for people on-site to tap into the needs at their own location.

Some companies spend millions to inspire, motivate, and retain their best employees, but their tactics often miss the mark—they aren't based on what really drives or motivates staff. It's important not to miss the mark! I mentioned earlier that there is no one-size-fits-all blanket solution for all organizations, and neither is there a single blanket solution *within* organizations. For example, one department may want to work later hours during the week for comp time later in the month, while another would rather take an extended lunch on certain days. It's not unheard of to put different benefits or motivators in place for different groups of employees.

START SMALL

Listening to your employees is the best way to start making positive changes to your culture. You can begin by scheduling a listening session, sending a survey, or conducting focus groups. Ask questions, such as "What do you like about work? What don't you like?" When employees trust you and know you care, they will give honest responses.

"I love my job. I love working with my teams," or "We don't have any flex time and I've got two kids at home. It's really stressful sometimes."

Once you've gathered feedback, figure out where you can quickly implement one or two easy changes and create big wins. Maybe you can change a policy or hire additional temporary help to reduce stress on your team. I suggest selecting and making some changes right away, because all too frequently companies plan for change and then fail to implement. If you can make two changes over the course of a few days or weeks, no matter how small, you'll get the ball rolling and create immediate momentum to keep moving forward.

Continue to think about what's needed at your company, your department, or organization, and continue with the transformation. Chances are your organization is in a good place and poised for growth, so you may only need to make a few modest changes to move from like to love. However, if you have a toxic environment, it's going to be a lot harder. You'll have to figure out exactly what is making the workplace that way.

As you make changes, measure the effect and iterate as needed. For example, if we were to measure the effectiveness and relevance of Beer Cart Friday at my company, we'd begin by asking, "What is our goal in offering this initiative, and is it effective?" It's important to gather solid evidence to determine whether employee engagement has improved—you need to measure results. You can gather evidence through employee satisfaction surveys and having ongoing discussions with team members. Find out how they feel about current initiatives, and whether or not they would refer a friend to come work for your company. You can also measure effectiveness through pure numbers and statistics. You can look at the rate of turnover, for example, and determine if it has increased or decreased. Numbers leave no gray areas and show the true impact of an initiative.

LISTEN TO FEEDBACK

My partner and I have been running a company for over thirty-three years and, at times, we can be set in our ways. However, we've come to embrace the fact that we must listen to employee feedback and make changes to meet their needs—this helps facilitate the move from like to love. Our employees made it known that we needed to provide more opportunities for work-life integration, and we've worked to accommodate their requests.

Our policies have become more flexible, and now we allow employees to work from home on certain days of the week or seasons of the year. To give an example, if someone has a project deadline coming up, they may want to work on it at home, without interruption. We offer paid-volunteer days, so people can serve nonprofit organizations in the community during regular work hours. This allows them to volunteer without having to use vacation days or personal time. We also offer comp time, and allow employees to take an additional number of days off.

END OF CHAPTER CHECKLIST/CHEAT SHEET

- Does your company seek feedback from your employees?

- Do you know what motivates your staff?

- Have you initiated any changes to bring more comfort and fun to the workplace?

- Do you respond quickly and effectively to employee requests?

- If you were to pick one thing to start positive change in your company, what would it be?

PART TWO

LIKE TO LOVE IN ACTION: DISCOVERY, TRANSFORMATION, AND RESPONSE

Chapter Six

DISCOVERY: WHAT'S REALLY HAPPENING?

Discovery is the first step in the "like to love" design process. The only way to know what's happening in your company is to ask. It sounds simple because it is. The first step is asking employees what they like, love, don't like, or even hate about the organization. Once you begin collecting data, themes will emerge. Chances are you already know what 80 percent of the responses will be, but the other 20 percent may surprise you.

The purpose of surveying your employees is to identify opportunities for improvement. Oftentimes, the solutions are simple. For example, if employees complain about the distance between the parking lot and the front door, the remedy could be getting a shuttle bus, or subsidizing Uber rides. This small, fixable issue could be affecting employee moods, but you can't do anything about it unless you ask!

KEY ELEMENTS OF DISCOVERY

There are three key elements used in the discovery phase:

- **Employee surveys and interviews.** These can be done on an individual level, and larger companies can also conduct focus groups.
- **Leadership interviews and work sessions.** These are used to identify and articulate key objectives, challenges, and opportunities.
- **Corporate culture audit.** Identifies cultural strengths, weaknesses, and gaps in communication.

The Nitrous Effect assists clients with conducting the discovery process, and it can be done in a number of different ways. Just like the process of implementing change, how you go about discovery depends on the size of your organization. A large company might need to do an employee satisfaction survey once a year, but in an office with three people, you know where everyone stands every day. In either case, a quick spot survey can be effective—this can be as simple as asking for "thumbs up" and "thumbs down" responses. Formal surveys have their place, but there's no need to send a twenty-page document each time you request feedback from employees.

Once you complete your initial discovery findings, leadership needs to ask, "Are there employee needs that aren't being met? Do we need to drive a change in behavior? Do we need to take a timeout, bring everyone together, and discuss issues?"

The more you can find out about your employees, teams, and customers, the better. In the discovery process, information is power—the more you know, the more you can take steps toward creating a healthy environment and culture of love.

LOOKING FOR TRENDS

I mentioned the buttons near our office exit that ask employees about their day—they choose green for "good" and red for "not-so-good." Of course, we hope for all greens because that means everyone is loving their work, but we don't panic over a couple of reds. However, if we get more than three, that tells leadership that something is up.

Not every company has to do a daily survey or pulse check, but we're a creative agency, so it's important for us to be aware of what's happening with our people. We monitor the results on a daily basis so we can look for trends. Trends could show up in terms of responses on certain days of the week, times of year, or in relation to the seasonality of our business. For example, in the first quarter, everyone was slammed with work, so we had a few reds. People were stressed because they were putting in extra hours and handling demanding clients, and this created a trend. We took action and did all we could to provide the best possible environment: we provided lunches, brought in freelancers, and encouraged people to talk to their supervisors more often.

I want to emphasize that trend identification isn't just limited to the organizational level—it can be done with departments, groups, teams, and individuals. If you see a trend with a particular employee, take the time to assess where they are in their career, year, month, or week. Perhaps they are overworked, or they have a personal issue that is affecting their work. You need to find out the root cause and work with them to restore a healthy level of engagement.

END OF CHAPTER CHECKLIST/CHEAT SHEET

- Do you know how your employees feel about working for your company?

- Are you using surveys, interviews, or conversations to discover how employees feel and the changes they'd like to see?

- Have you noticed particular trends in employee responses and feedback?

- Are you implementing any changes based on employee feedback?

Chapter Seven

CARE: WE ALL DESERVE IT

Do you remember the first of the five basic needs to build emotional connections and relationships?

You genuinely care about me.

Employees want and need to be cared about, and the benefits you offer are an important "care tool." As part of the discovery phase mentioned in the previous chapter, I suggest you conduct a "benefits and perks" survey and analysis. Every company has their own ideas when it comes to appropriate benefits and perks. These are often based on their industry, region, and other factors.

Your benefits and perks survey should differentiate between benefits that are vital, such as health insurance and paid vacations, and those that are considered "extras." We know it's not essential to have Beer Cart Fridays, but it's a nice perk! Employees like to take a break, hang out with coworkers, and have a beer. Doing all you can to provide essential benefits—plus some extras—will ensure your company remains competitive in the marketplace.

CULTURE OF CHANGE

While pay matters, it isn't always the reason people accept or reject a job offer. Our CPG agency consults with many companies, and we see a common thread: people want to work for an outstanding company, and they want to like their coworkers.

Company values and employee engagement are key factors as to why people choose an employer. It's therefore of the utmost importance to keep a finger on the pulse of your organization. If your company needs a culture change, you'll have to design and push initiatives to make it happen. This might require some uncomfortable or courageous conversations with employees and the leadership team. Sometimes, change can rub against the grain at first.

A startup business has an advantage over an established company because it's brand new. Startups have the opportunity to design their culture from scratch and decide how they want it to take shape. Existing companies must *change* company culture, and that's hard work, but our "like to love" design process will guide you through it.

CASE STUDY: L. KEELEY CONSTRUCTION

L. Keeley Construction in St. Louis demonstrates that they value connection in their communities through a program called #KeeleyCares. This program encourages employees to become involved in local charities and their events. They have a family-oriented mindset and culture, and host various employee-family events throughout the year. They also have a goal of bringing people together who may not work together on a daily basis, so they provide lunches and all-employee happy hours.

According to Rusty Keeley, CEO:

> Being a Keeley'n is about more than what we do while in the office, in the field, or on a jobsite—it's also about making an impact in the community. We have a collaborative spirit that makes our team members love being a part of the Keeley family. We've facilitated a culture of giving back through a program called #KeeleyCares. Recently, 250 of our people participated in events like Pedal the Cause and JDRF walks, and they helped raise over $75,000.
>
> We illustrate our values and mission on the walls at our L. Keeley Construction headquarters in St. Louis. Our "Wall

of Compassion" holds the logos of more than twenty charities our company and team members have committed to helping. Beyond a hashtag, #KeeleyCares represents a way of life, and we're proud to represent it.

We have a family-oriented mindset that extends to our team members' families—we put the well-being of our Keeley'ns and their families first. We host many family-friendly outings, including Six Flags Day, St. Louis Cardinals Day, Breakfast with Santa, a safety fair, and many others throughout the year. We want everyone to feel the strength of our core values.

As the CEO, I personally send an email to each and every Keeley'n on their birthday, reminding them they are a valuable part of our team. We cater lunches on a regular basis, and we host happy hour events to encourage team members who don't usually work together to get acquainted.

LUVFEST is also a great "Keeleyism." This began as a toast, and it's transitioned into a movement. This is a company dinner where each Keeley'n stands to give a toast. We recognize people and tell success stories, and that gets everyone thinking about the special company we are creating.

CASE STUDY: ULTA BEAUTY

Ulta Beauty does a tremendous job of developing their

people. They promote from within because they want to motivate their employees and hire the best leaders, and they provide potential career paths to demonstrate their care. They contribute to breast cancer research programs to broaden their positive impact on women, and have provided help to employees in the midst of natural disasters and catastrophes.

According to Raquel Frankenreider, senior vice president, store operations:

> Whenever our senior leaders travel, they make a point of scheduling town-hall-style meetings with store associates whenever possible. We pull as many associates as we can from the field to share their insights and concerns, and to address their questions. They also follow up to offer solutions to challenges they face. If they have a question or concern that can't be answered on-site, they compile and share the answers at a later date. We're also invested in employee growth and development, and we pride ourselves on promoting from within.

According to Kecia Steelman, chief store operations officer:

> Care is part of what the company stands for. We're all about open communication, and we take care of each other like family. During the recent hurricane in Houston, we discovered that some Ulta Beauty employees were misplaced

due to the disaster. We rented a bus to transport those individuals and their families to hotels. We covered the cost of the rooms, and provided gift cards and vouchers.

We also had employees who lost everything in the California fires, and we took care of them as well. It didn't matter if the employee was a manager, full-time, or part-time—we didn't think twice about it. It was the right thing to do, because we're a family.

CASE STUDY: SOUTHWEST AIRLINES

Southwest Airlines' leadership demonstrates a high level of care for their employees, and the employees also demonstrate care for one another.

According to Cheryl Hughey, managing director of culture:

"People don't care about what you know, until they know you care." This is one of my favorite quotes, and it speaks volumes about your actions. What is it that you're doing that demonstrates care? When you show that you care, it creates a strong bond with others within an organization. It also creates an effort and attitude from employees that says, "I'm willing to do and give more, because I know my organization, leaders, and company care about me."

This type of effort only happens when you really know your

employees. Knowing them means you understand what's happening in their lives inside and outside of work. A great Southwest example that speaks to this is our internal customer care team (ICC). ICC was formed from the idea that leaders need to know what is going on in the lives of the employees, and we need to acknowledge anything that is going on, good or bad. They could be family issues, illnesses, or marital stress. We know it's important for leaders to be informed, and to acknowledge and help with these issues in the most appropriate way.

We also demonstrate care through our Catastrophic Fund. Peers and employees can deduct money from their paychecks to be given to employees who are in catastrophic situations. We saw this firsthand when employees had needs after the hurricanes. We had our first telethon to talk about the fund, and the company matched employee donations dollar-for-dollar. Within twenty-four hours, the money was in the hands of the employees in need.

END OF CHAPTER CHECKLIST/CHEAT SHEET

- Do you know whether or not your employees feel the company cares about them?

- Do you provide only essential benefits, or do you offer some extras and perks to ensure that your company remains competitive in the marketplace? If so, what are they?

- How does your company demonstrate that values and employee engagement are key factors when potential new hires are looking into your organization?

- Does your company need a culture change that emphasizes caring?

Chapter Eight

TRUST: BUILDING IT IS NO LONGER OPTIONAL

What tools take care of the second basic need: *I trust you and you trust me?*

We know that people want companies to be transparent, and for there to be a mutual trust between employer and employee. To make this process run smoothly, we encourage companies we work with as clients to implement a Shared Understanding and Values initiative. This kind of initiative serves to build values and expectations through day-to-day interactions within a company.

A Shared Understanding and Values initiative is leaders being open with employees and building the values of the organization into daily interactions. As a leader, you must demonstrate through your words and actions that you trust them, and they in turn will trust you. They see the way you manage and represent the company, and the things you do every day—they view your work ethic as an example, and they want clear, concise language and communication from leadership. Employees have expectations of their company, and their experience must match those expectations—that's how you build trust.

For example, at our agencies, we have shifted financial work to the team-leader level. Previously, upper-level managers or directors would need to approve certain transactions, but by empowering team leaders to take care of them, we've built trust with the employees who do the work every day.

We strive to build trust as much as possible between employees and the organization. However, we can't succeed in this endeavor if we ignore the fact that sometimes there is a lack of trust between individual employees, departments, or divisions. It's possible one department doesn't trust another because that department is chronically late for work or fails to deliver on their promises. It's important to place a focus on building trust internally, on multiple levels, as well.

IMPROVING OUR GAME

At The Nitrous Effect, we align around what we call our

"big rocks." These are our goals, objectives, rules, protocols, roles, responsibilities, resources, templates, and schedules. We clearly communicate these, and then we highlight and amplify our engagement activities. We might make an announcement through a short-burst communication or on Slack. If we need to discuss a big initiative, we'll have a company-wide meeting. We have weekly meetings and regular project meetings, so there's no confusion about our big rocks and goals. We make every effort to communicate frequently.

I mentioned the example earlier of football teams watching game films to analyze their plays and figure out what to do differently next time. At our company, we also study our strengths, weaknesses, and the end results of initiatives. Our desired outcome is love, happier people, and an increase in profits, but if these things aren't happening, we need to watch the game film and revisit the playbook. We need to uncover what is lacking in our current processes, what needs to be changed, and whether or not we need additional resources.

CASE STUDIES

Let's take a look at how Ulta Beauty and Virgin Hotels respond to employee requests for improvements, and how Virgin wants guests and team members to feel good after their experience at their hotels.

According to Raquel Frankenreider, Ulta's senior vice president of store operations:

> We want to empower our associates, and we do this by providing them with the data, tools, and training to effectively run their business. All of our leaders are similar in that they give their teams the autonomy to make decisions.
>
> We're extremely inclusive, and we listen to our teams—they talk, we listen, and we make changes based on their feedback. In fact, our CEO has an email address specifically for feedback, and we have meetings throughout the year to ask for it. Our managers solicit feedback from their teams on a weekly basis, and they send information to leadership, as well.
>
> We recently received feedback from our store teams that they found it challenging to access sales results. They had to follow a series of steps and pull fifteen different reports from the system. Based on their feedback, we created an all-inclusive mobile dashboard. Also, our associates were unable to post-void transactions, so we implemented that capability into our system.

According to Kecia Steelman, Ulta's chief store operations officer:

I always seek to understand. You don't know what happened before you walked through the door. An associate could be facing a problem inside or outside of work. Slowing down and being observant goes a long way. My style of leadership is not command-and-control. It's "What can I do to make your job easier? What are the obstacles that are in your way?" If I can help make them successful, then we're successful as an organization.

VIRGIN HOTELS

According to Clio Knowles, VP of people at Virgin Hotels:

Obviously, we want to create a culture of trust. We provide a generous benefits package, listen to employee requests and do our best to follow through with solutions. We just conducted an employee survey, and we have new action plans to implement based on the issues that were raised. For example, our teammates said they didn't like our cafeteria, so we responded by making improvements to change their experience. They know they can share their concerns, and even their complaints, when they see that changes really do get implemented as a result.

We share recognition through our People Platform system. We call it the "Valentine's Program," because you can send the love to other teammates. We also make sure we're transparent and share survey results—this is so everyone can understand where we're hitting it out of the park, and where we might be lacking.

We aim for everyone to leave our hotels feeling better than when they came in. This isn't just about the guests feeling better—we want this for our teammates, too. We want them to learn new information and have a good time before they go home. We want our investors to feel better because they know they've made more money than they would have with another brand. And, this sounds a little over the top, but, we want the planet to feel better—Virgin Hotels focuses on sustainability. Every day, we focus on this cornerstone question: "If I do this, will people leave feeling better?" If the answer is yes, keep going. If the answer is no, what's an alternative option? That question is our guiding principle.

END OF CHAPTER CHECKLIST/CHEAT SHEET

- Are you building trust through day-to-day interactions across the company?

- Do you promote a company culture of shared understanding and values?

- Do you demonstrate through words and actions that you trust your employees? Do you strive to build a culture of trust among individuals, departments, and divisions? How?

Chapter Nine

LISTENING AND COMMUNICATION: IF YOU TUNE OUT, SO WILL THEY

The third basic need of employees: *You listen to me.*

For companies and organizations, the big question here is *how* do you listen? There are countless ways to listen today. Communication technology is ever evolving. Email and intranets have given way to social media, mobile apps, workplace apps like Slack, and other internal applications. Among Millennials and Gen Z, apps are the preferred method of communication. They offer convenient, cost-effective ways to let employees lead conversations, share their struggles and celebrations, and chat about topics relevant to their work.

Technology can make the process of listening convenient, but I don't suggest you solely rely on it. There are other, more personal ways to dig deep and find out how employees really feel. These methods include, but are not limited to, feedback forums, pop-up surveys, and formal sentiment surveys.

A DEEPER CONNECTION

Feedback forums are a place to connect with employees, inform them about company affairs, collect information, and hold open discussions. These can be conducted as town hall sessions, regular staff meetings, and lunch-and-learns. You must demonstrate the value of these forums by responding to employee input and taking action when required.

Pop-up surveys are short, simple, and playful. They're strategically designed to gather insight and build conversation. When we conduct these, we always report the results and insights with employees right away. When you take in feedback, whether from employees or clients, you should share the information you gathered. This lets them know their opinions have been heard, and they can find out what their peers have to say.

DIFFICULT OR UNCOMFORTABLE COMMUNICATION

It's oddly refreshing when a company applauds the uncomfortable.

For example, Zappos has a company policy that if an employee decides they aren't a good fit for the company, they are encouraged to step up and communicate it. If they do step up, follow through, and leave within ninety days, they receive a bonus. As strange as it may seem, this strategy helps the company minimize the problem of employee disengagement and ensures there is a cultural fit between Zappos and its employees.

Company leaders will get difficult questions from their people every now and then—it's a healthy consequence of growth. Ulta Beauty is unique in that they appreciate when someone asks a tough or controversial question during a town hall meeting.

According to Kecia Steelman, chief store operations officer:

> If someone asks a tough question during a town hall meeting, we celebrate. We thank them for asking the question, because we know other people in the room may not have had the courage to ask it.

At CPG, we also welcome our people to put the pressure on, because we want to be transparent in everything we say and do. We realize that sometimes difficult conversations are necessary to resolve problems.

END OF CHAPTER CHECKLIST/CHEAT SHEET

- What communication technology and tools do you use to listen to your employees?

- Do you welcome difficult or uncomfortable questions?

- Are you always looking for new ways to engage employees in communication?

- Have you ever used feedback forums, pop-up surveys, or formal sentiment surveys to connect with staff?

Chapter Ten

EMPOWERMENT AND RECOGNITION: MORE THAN AN ID NUMBER

In this chapter, we'll examine recognition tools—the ones that correspond to the fourth basic need: *You appreciate me for who I am and you tell me so.*

To properly address the topic of recognition, we first need to discuss the importance of diversity in the workplace and the role it plays in the transition from like to love. The people who are qualified for jobs in your organization will come from a wide variety of backgrounds, and so, in order to attract and retain them as employees, you must embrace and value diversity, and *make it known* that you do. Walk the walk.

Diversity is not a term that only refers to different races and ethnicities—it also encompasses demographics including educational background, age, economic class, and work and life experience. No two people are the same, and having an array of perspectives only benefits your organization. A commitment to diversity not only attracts a variety of people into your workforce, it also expands the possibility of gaining new clients and customers.

Diversity is also invaluable because it provides the opportunity to listen to and learn from a broad range of people and experiences. It creates the perfect blend of professional development and engagement, moving people from like to love.

SHARING POINTS OF VIEW

There's a wide range of tools you can use to empower and recognize diversity of opinion, experience, and perspective at your company. We believe companies should use social apps not just for standard company communication, but also for shout-outs, giving recognition, and helping people stay in touch.

At The Nitrous Effect, we've introduced a program called "True Selves." This program invites and incentivizes individuals to build a personal story and share about their lives and personal perspectives. This highlights connections, similarities, and other unique details to promote company and coworker appreciation for diversity. True Selves can be implemented through an internal social app or shared physical space.

The more we are able to share with our companies, clients, and employees, the more we can appreciate each of them as individuals. We have several clients who have weekly employee celebrations to highlight connections, similarities, and interesting details about their people.

GRATEFUL GRAFFITI

As wonderful and convenient as apps and technology are, they can't replace the experience of a shared physical space, a unique spot where people can collaborate.

Such sharing of thoughts, or "grateful graffiti," can be physical or digital—I describe it as "phygital." It's another tool we use to recognize colleagues, and we recommend it to our clients. When people enter our office, they see a giant chalkboard wall. This is where we write shout-outs, recognize our employee of the week, and write other things worth celebrating.

Our space has a wall with our company values painted on it—this is where we invite employees to build their personal story and share their points of view for the True

Selves program. It's also a prime meeting spot for parties and events, and we take our company photos there. Leadership works hard to make sure we have gatherings to celebrate big wins for the company, as well as individual life changes and victories. If an employee has a baby, or wins a client or an award, we celebrate the individual and their team. Recognizing our people and celebrating these victories not only creates a fun work environment, it has moved our employees from like to love very quickly.

The way we conduct celebrations also sets the precedent for the rest of the organization. The first thing people do in our Monday morning staff meetings is give shout-outs to recognize one another and show gratitude. "I want to thank Jason for helping me with this escalated issue last week. He was awesome!" When someone receives praise in front of other people, they feel great, and it gets them further into "love" mode.

OTHER WAYS TO RECOGNIZE EMPLOYEES

L. Keeley Construction gives out fun company swag like logo socks and shirts to get people engaged with the company. If you love where you work, you'll love wearing the company logo! Southwest Airlines gives a branded gift to employees after one year of service, and they acknowledge other employee milestones in various ways. This might seem a bit "touchy-feely," but this type of recognition is important to transition your employees from like to love.

The Nitrous Effect agencies like to recognize employees in many ways. We don't always do something formal—we often give what we call "surprise and delight" rewards, like an extra day off, or a prime parking spot. We also award people with a day to play hooky and go to the horse races. We do all we can to integrate personal lives into the workplace by making celebrations for birthdays and other occasions a part of our culture.

END OF CHAPTER CHECKLIST/CHEAT SHEET

- Do you value diversity at your organization? How do you show it?

- Do you encourage your employees to share their personal stories and unique points of view?

- Do you use a wide range of communication tools to empower and recognize your employees?

- Do you celebrate the victories and successes of individuals and teams in your organization?

Chapter Eleven

MEANINGFUL PURPOSE: WHAT OTHER KIND IS THERE?

There are a few different empowerment and recognition tools that will help you meet the fifth basic need: *We share a meaningful purpose.*

MISSION MOTIVATION WORKSHOP

The Mission Motivation Workshop takes an organization through the process of creating a clear, inspired mission. This process can be especially beneficial for newer companies that have yet to articulate their mission, vision, and values. It's also helpful for established companies that have executives whose perspectives are not in alignment. If leadership is misaligned, then the organization will be as well.

When senior leaders aren't in agreement about what matters most, it will ultimately result in poor employee performance and financial results. Companies need to articulate their mission, vision, and values in inspiring ways, and they need to gather input from many employees to do so. Remember, employees want and need to be heard. That doesn't mean they get the final vote, but leaders need to listen and take their feedback into consideration.

CONNECTING WITH THE MISSION

A company's mission isn't merely a series of words that form a statement. It's an expression of why everyone at the company is working together, and that they are working toward a common goal. I recommend that companies remind themselves of their mission on a daily basis, and renew it when necessary. This is an important part of their commitment to serve their brand and customers.

CASE STUDY: L. KEELEY CONSTRUCTION

As a small, closely held family business, L. Keeley Construction is very up front about its mission and purpose. The company promotes a collaborative family spirit among its employees through family-oriented events, special honorary lunches, and celebrations of individual and team success. The company's core values are reflected in safety fairs and community give-back programs, such as #KeeleyCares and Pedal the Cause.

L. Keeley Construction uses the acronym "PRIDE" to capture their values: People, Respect, Integrity, Discipline, and Empowerment. They illustrate these values and their mission on a Wall of Compassion at company headquarters, and they also display the logos of more than twenty charities to which the company and team members are committed. The company's LUVFEST dinner is an opportunity for each employee to offer a toast recognizing other staff members and their success stories. Because leadership promotes the company mission on a daily basis, employees are happy in their jobs and love where they work.

According to Rusty Keeley, the company's CEO:

> Not only do we have our purpose and values proudly displayed in our offices, we give every Keeley'n a card to put in their wallet and keep on their person. We start many meetings and conversations by discussing our values and mission. Most importantly, we always focus on what our values and mission mean to each individual. We want to know everyone's "why," and how it ties back to our mission.

Virgin Hotels is another prime example of a company that embraces its mission. Based on the "the three Ps:" People,

Planet, and Partners, their We Care Program is an internal call to action in which employees choose and promote their favorite causes. People can pitch campaigns in outrageous ways and recruit followers. Southwest Airlines also articulates their vision clearly and connects that vision to the company's culture and history whenever possible.

How do you embrace and communicate your company's mission, vision, and purpose?

THE BUSINESS IQ INITIATIVE

A truly engaged workplace requires that every employee understand the company's mission, vision, goals, value proposition, differentiation, and the significance of their roles. It's simple to share these with employees and to produce synergy, but it's hard to believe how many companies fail to clearly articulate them.

If these elements haven't been established in your organization, I encourage you to start making them apparent now. If you have yet to formulate a mission, vision, or solid goals, start by asking yourself and your leadership team, "Why?"

Why are we doing this? Why are we in business? Why is this important to us?

Once you know the answers and have clearly developed

the language for them, communicate them to everyone, and I mean *everyone*. From receptionists to the CFO, from mailroom employees to the CMO, from accounting clerks to the CSO—they all need to know that what they do matters, and they need to know *why*.

As part of our Business IQ Initiative, we often move our up-and-coming or senior employees around the building. Someone could work in finance this month, and then work in operations next month—there are endless learning opportunities. This type of job sharing and cross-training can even become a formal workshop or class. The rock stars in your organization want to learn, advance, and be promoted, and providing these opportunities will help them love your organization.

This initiative must also include transparent communication of information that is often kept away from employees. You can't tell them everything, but you can share about 90 percent—that's what we do. We let them know how we won a particular client or account, or why we didn't get business from a certain company. If we bring in a new employee after we told them we were holding off on adding new staff, we explain why. In fact, the only information we withhold is about salaries and bonuses. We've leaned heavily into this level of transparency over the past few years, and there has been an overall improvement in our culture. I don't know what we were so afraid of before!

GENERATION GAP

I consider my business partner, David Stillman, author of *When Generations Collide* and *Gen Z @ Work*, to be the foremost expert on generational differences. He has an eighteen-year-old Generation Z son, and he's researched and collected data on generational differences for years. He and his son have regular speaking engagements with chief communications officers because they have information and personal insight to share on the ever-present generation gap. David will share some of his expertise with you in Chapter Thirteen: "Love Potions for Engagement Excellence."

The generations that are currently in the workforce are Baby Boomers, Gen Xers, Gen Ys, Millennials, Gen Zs, and there will soon be another group! Some have experienced war, others saw their parents lose their jobs and homes in the Great Recession of 2007 and 2008—each generation has had different life experiences.

The generation gap greatly influences how to best communicate with employees. Each generation has different expectations, and their communication preferences vary. At our company, the age of our employees ranges from twenty-three to sixty-five. Everyone gets along well, but the twenty-three-year-olds use Snapchat and the sixty-five-year-olds don't. If we want people to love their workplace, it's important for us to provide more than one option for communication.

INITIATIVES IN ACTION

We didn't invent this concept, but we love it. It's the "Tour of Duty" initiative from the book *The Alliance*, by Reid Hoffman, cofounder of LinkedIn. As we begin to consult more and more clients, we've found many of them are open to using this initiative. The idea is that employees commit to a job or role for a clearly defined, limited amount of time, subject to extensions. At the end of that period, employees review their level of commitment, and they either renew it for another tour or move on to another opportunity.

The Tour of Duty is similar to what they do in the military. They send a captain to Afghanistan for six months, he serves his tour of duty, then afterward, he might be able to pick some other place to go. This is how our Tour of Duty initiative works, and we've had outstanding results.

Imagine that your boss gives you a marketing project, and by the time you're finished, you're completely bored with marketing. The Tour of Duty allows your boss to say, "I want you to help me for six months, and this is how we will grade your performance. At the end of the six months, we will reconnect and see if you want to continue with this, or if you're ready to move on to something else." To give you a specific example, my senior project manager is currently serving a one-year Tour of Duty. We want him to grow with our organization, so at the end of the year, we'll sit down and say, "What do you want to do next?" He might say, "I'll do this for one more year, but next year, I want to be a video producer." If that's the case, we'll accommodate his request—we'll get him there. The Tour of Duty initiative can help you keep employees engaged and fired up about working for your organization or retain an employee who has one foot halfway out the door.

In a SlideShare on LinkedIn, Reid Hoffman says, "Employers, managers, and employees need a new relationship framework where they make promises to each other they can keep. Stop thinking of employees as family or free agents. Start thinking of employees as allies on a tour of duty. Employment should be an alliance: a mutually beneficial deal with explicit terms between independent players. Employer and employee develop a relationship based on how they can add value to each other. Employees invest in the company's success. The company invests in the employees' market value. The result is a mutually beneficial alliance instead of a transactional relationship."[5]

As you can tell, 90 percent of what's suggested in this book is very simple, and many of these strategies cost little money. You just need a roadmap. I want to get you thinking about what needs to be done so your employees will love working for you, and to get your customers to

---

5   Hoffman, Reid. LinkedIn SlideShare, https://www.slideshare.net/reidhoffman/
     the-alliance-a-visual-summary/53-For_example_Over_the_next.

love working with *them*. If there's a roadblock, you can move it out of the way.

END OF CHAPTER CHECKLIST/CHEAT SHEET

- Do you articulate your company's mission, vision, and purpose in inspiring ways?

- Are your employees engaged in the workplace in a way that they can understand and promote the company's mission, vision, and values through their roles?

- Do you review your company's mission daily and align it with your company's culture?

- Do you have a roadmap to engage your employees in ways that they love working in your organization?

Chapter Twelve

DIALOGUE, RESPONSE, ITERATION, AND MEASUREMENT: PROCESS IS YOUR PRODUCT

As a company leader, you interact with employees every day, and sometimes you need to move your people to action. How can you ensure that your interventions take employees and customers from like to love?

First, monitor progress closely. At The Nitrous Effect, we meet and talk often. We pay attention to the results of our pulse checks and employee responses to the "How's Your Day?" button. We constantly monitor the progress of everything we do so we can be proactive and make adjustments along the way.

If you realize a program you've implemented isn't working, tweak it immediately. Speed is of the utmost importance. Many old-line companies conduct employee satisfaction surveys only once a year, but the average Millennial has 144 interactions per day! You can't ask people a question once a year—you have to ask it every day.

HOW DO YOU MEASURE SUCCESS?

Every company is unique, and each one handles success metrics differently. What are your company's objections? Have you seen an improvement against your baseline scores? How do you take the pulse of your employees? Do you measure employee satisfaction? Once you decide what needs to be done, determine what types of measurements would be most effective for your organization.

I mentioned pop-up surveys in Chapter Nine. In a similar fashion, you can conduct quick employee-satisfaction surveys. They provide immediate feedback and can be delivered in a variety of formats. Depending on the level of specificity you seek, these can be multiple-choice, written answers, or a combination of both. We like to do employee brainstorming, and we've found this survey method to be effective for clients and for our company. Instead of three leaders sitting in a room making decisions, we have the entire company giving us feedback and helping us launch initiatives.

We've also launched a concept called the "Idea Kitchen." This is CPG's proprietary name for the process, but other companies might call it an "idea jam." This is a creative way for employees to address a problem for a client or find new ideas and solutions. Depending on the desired outcome, they can be quick, half-hour, internal sessions or full-day events.

For example, let's say The Nitrous Effect is pitching a new client. We bring ten staff members together from different departments or different walks of life. Then we conduct an idea jam on how to win this client's business. We've also done idea jams with external clients. We did one with a large fashion company that was going through a time of transition. They aimed to accomplish tremendous goals, but the implementation wasn't going well, so we had a problem-solving idea jam with a thousand people at their headquarters.

The process began with a half-hour town hall session with the CEO to set the tone. Then, to gather innovative solutions, we brought together different employees for brainstorming—everyone got a minute and a half to share ideas on a whiteboard we named the "board of inspiration." There was representation from security, accounting, fashion, and even the CMO. Everyone loved that their ideas were being included. "Wow, I'm an accounting clerk, but you're listening to my ideas. That's great because I feel like I know fashion, too." The company wasn't just gathering ideas; they were also demonstrating that they listen to and care about their employees.

Another type of idea jam you're probably familiar with is crowdsourcing. We use this as another way to help our clients gather ideas, and we also do this ourselves. I might say to an employee, "Get twelve of your friends together tomorrow night. Here's a Starbucks gift card. Go out for coffee and treats, brainstorm, and come up with three ideas for this new client." Or maybe we'll present a new product to the group and ask for their feedback: "What do you think of these new shades of lipstick?"

CONSISTENCY IS KEY

At The Nitrous Effect, we want our agencies to be consistent in measurements of employee success, so we've gotten rid of long-term annual reviews. This doesn't mean *you* need to get rid of them, but you must have another method in place to regularly evaluate employees. Our agencies are working to streamline a process that used to take a year and get it down to a few seconds—we're implementing a system that measures employee performance on a weekly or daily basis. If an employee isn't doing well, or if they haven't turned in an assignment, they might get an unfavorable rating immediately. People want simple, and that's what we aim to deliver.

THE IMPORTANCE OF EXIT INTERVIEWS

When an employee leaves your company, it can make you feel like you've failed in some way, but that may not be the case. When someone leaves one of our agencies, we make it a priority to conduct an exit interview. An employee might have a reason for leaving that has nothing to do with the job, and we need to gather that information. Likewise, if they are leaving because they felt they had a terrible experience, we need that feedback as well. We want and need honest feedback, and we gather it consistently. We use that information for qualitative measurements, and to create action plans for improvement.

END OF CHAPTER CHECKLIST/CHEAT SHEET

- Have you set a baseline and measured the impact from like to love initiatives?

- Do you provide regular feedback to employees—more frequently than once a year?

- In your performance reviews, do you ask your employees what they love to do?

- How do you get the group, department, or company to immediately brainstorm a problem in half an hour?

- Would an "idea jam" be beneficial at your organization? What types of issues could this help you address?

Chapter Thirteen

LOVE POTIONS FOR ENGAGEMENT EXCELLENCE

I've shared ideas and best practices from CPG and some of our clients in this book. Now, I'd like to share what leaders of some of the top, most engaging companies do. In this chapter, they'll discuss what they've done to achieve success, how they moved employees from like to love, and how they keep them there. They've set an example and they lead the way in engagement excellence. I've had the privilege of cultivating relationships with leaders like Maxine K. Clark of Build-A-Bear Workshop, Mark Moses of CEO Coaching, and Robert Glazer of Acceleration Partners. I'm excited to share their words with you! We'll conclude this chapter with some insight on navigating the generational gap in the workplace from generations expert and best-selling author David Stillman.

MAXINE K. CLARK, CEO OF CLARK-FOX FAMILY FOUNDATION, FOUNDER OF BUILD-A-BEAR WORKSHOP

Maxine K. Clark is a well-known American innovator and leader. Not only is she the CEO of the Clark-Fox Family Foundation and Founder of Build-A-Bear Workshop, she is Inspirator of The Delmar Divine, a high-impact real estate initiative in St. Louis; managing partner of Prosper Women's Capital; and executive in residence at Washington University in St. Louis for the John M. Olin School of Business. Here, she shares how Build-A-Bear-Workshop began, and why the employees love the company so much.

BUILD-A-BEAR WORKSHOP: THE EARLY DAYS

I had the idea for Build-A-Bear in January of 1997, and we opened the first store in October of that same year. We started with four people in the corporate office and thirty in-store employees. However, we had to keep hiring more people because business was through the roof.

Our company and business concept were unique. Nothing like it had existed before, so there was an overwhelming response from applicants because it was so new—people applied for jobs at the first store not knowing what they were getting into, but they were excited. Many applicants had sales experience, and others were current and former teachers, nurses, counselors, or social workers who enjoyed working with children.

We knew from the beginning that our employees had to be a good fit for the store. Our people had to be right for the roles and what we wanted to accomplish. We appreciated the variety of applicants, because we needed a wide range of skills and interests. For example, a former teacher was perfect to work the retail floor but not for the role of manager—someone with business experience would be a better fit.

As we grew, the responsibilities for managers did as well. We had up to thirty-five people on the payroll at a single store, so we needed to hire people who were capable of overseeing a large number of employees and creating efficient schedules. At one point, I wanted to promote a teacher to a management position, but her strength was helping the customers. No matter how wonderful the employee, we had to keep in mind that those who were good with children wouldn't necessarily make the best managers.

Even in those early days, I saw love in and from the team. At clothing retail stores, employees are expected to purchase and wear the clothing to work, but those expectations didn't apply to us. Our main focus was on how we could make children smile, rather than how much money we could make, and the employees loved that. We just hired "huggable" people—that was a trait we looked for in our candidates, and we replicated that practice in every store. There was no formal description for a Build-A-Bear employee; they just had to be themselves and have fun.

TRAINING AND DEVELOPMENT

To immerse our managers in our culture, we take them through a special training program when they are first hired, called "The Way of the Bear." It takes them through the experience of being a "bear," or an employee in our company. It shows them our story, and the *why* behind what we do. We also want them to see they are working for a company that cares about their lives outside of work, so this course encourages them to be better so they can enjoy their *whole* lives. People are often transformed after they finish the training!

In the world of retail, the rate of turnover can be close to 100 percent. Build-A-Bear has very little turnover—hardly any at all, really. We offer competitive pay, and people simply want to work for us. They enjoy working here, and they also have ample opportunity to move up the ladder. People know they can eventually become a manager at their location or at another store in the US. Build-A-Bear provides a lot of ongoing training—it's our way of "hugging" the employees.

CULTURE

We had no idea that Build-A-Bear would expand into a successful, international business. We simply wanted to create a fun store where children could enjoy themselves. The people we hired made the store—they are the ones who created our culture.

Our goal of having fun sparked an idea from a teacher who worked for us part-time: the heart ceremony. When a child builds a bear, they make a wish and place a heart inside of it, and this teacher created a ceremony for it. He had fun with it and trained everyone at his location. At first, the ceremony was only run at one store, but it caught on quickly at every location and became part of our culture. It was such an awesome idea because it contributed to the fun. In fact, people loved the ceremony so much, we ran out of hearts and now have to stock triple the previous amount!

Another unique part of our culture is the Build-A-Bear box. Our bears go home in a large cardboard box, and the outside is like a coloring book. Children brought the boxes back to the store to show employees how they had colored them. We didn't know this product feature would become a key part of our culture.

We've also made hugs a part of who we are. It's often frowned upon and viewed as unprofessional in corporate settings to give hugs, but we love them. When someone can't express their feelings, sometimes giving or receiving a hug is all they need. And there are times when the giver discovers they needed the hug just as much as the recipient!

LIKE TO LOVE

We enjoy having kids as customers, but we also want to connect with them. Participation in fundraisers like "College Bound" or "Teach for America" allows us to connect with the kids beyond their time in the stores. We want to know their stories and once we hear them, we're hooked and love them even more.

All of the love and action is in the stores, so we work to replicate that in the corporate office. We make sure the customer is always present and we read their letters at our meetings. We constantly add new people to the company, so every Monday we do something called "Shake and How You Wiggle." Everyone sits on the floor in a meeting room and we introduce ourselves. We also do fun icebreakers and get-to-know-you questions, like, "What's your favorite ice cream flavor?" And "If you could be any zoo animal, which would you be, and why?" We have up to seventy-five people in one room answering these questions.

Not only is this a great way to get to know new hires, you

learn something new every week about the people you've been working with. It's a fun way to connect and cut through hierarchies. It shows that we're all human beings, working together, gives employees a chance to see who we are, and gives them the opportunity to be themselves.

We also use "Bear Language" to shape and live our brand identity. We say things like, "Don't be 'em-Bear-ased,'" or "Beauty is in the Eye of the 'Bear-Holder.'" We have signs up everywhere with these phrases, even in the bathrooms. These techniques are corny, but they work!

FINAL WORDS

We believe our business is a canvas; a picture has been drawn, but it's incomplete. We describe what the full picture should look like in general terms, but employees have the freedom to color inside or outside the lines. The picture must resemble our expectations but they make it their own, and they can make it even bigger.

Let's say I drew the picture and used red, blue, and yellow. Somewhere in there, we needed to put in pink and purple and we allowed the employees to add those colors. We want everyone to make a contribution to the picture, whether behind the scenes or front and center— we want employees to fill in the blanks. The company has become bigger than I ever imagined, but my goal is for the company to be one of the top places to work in America, even after I'm gone. For me, that would be the ultimate accomplishment.

MARK MOSES, FOUNDING PARTNER AND CEO OF CEO COACHING INTERNATIONAL, FORMER CEO OF CAPITAL PLATINUM GROUP

Mark Moses, author of *Make Big Happen: How to Live, Work, and Give Big*, is a highly successful serial entrepreneur and top business coach. He's an energized keynote speaker, advises entrepreneurs and leaders toward extraordinary results, and regularly facilitates annual planning sessions for companies.

THE PLATINUM EXPERIENCE

When I was CEO of Platinum Capital, a mortgage banking firm, we had an incredible culture—everyone worked on the floor. One of our values was to have fun and the environment was engaging. We found that people performed better when they were having fun. If they didn't want to be there, we didn't want to have them there but if they wanted to work with us, we showed them a good time. Our employees loved their jobs so much, they kept referring friends to come work with us. We began a new division as a small firm with four people, and through referrals, we ended up with 275 employees in eighteen months.

Our people loved the culture. We did fun activities all the time. We played "Let's Make a Deal," and I pretended to be Monty Hall. We gave away awesome, crazy prizes, as well as some gag gifts. We also offered unique incentives. For example, the top salesperson got to drive a black convertible Mercedes 500 SL for a month. This prize fueled the fire, and everyone was in competition to win it. The competition was so fierce, no one ever won the prize two months in a row. We loved the drive that was fueled by the prize, and the fact that it led to a massive increase in sales.

We had a party every Friday afternoon and a "theme day" every month, where everyone would dress up according to the theme. We also decorated our office once per quarter, and created contests around these themes. We decorated the office to look like San Francisco, a cruise ship, and Las Vegas. For the Las Vegas theme, the office looked like a huge casino and if we beat our goal that quarter, we were going to take the entire company (three hundred people) to Vegas. We hit our goal on the very last day of the contest, so we all went to Vegas and had a blast. This got people fired up and made Platinum a cool and fun place to work.

Platinum became one of the top-performing mortgage companies in the US because we were driven by people who loved what they did, and we loved doing it along with them. To this day, when I wish former employees a Happy Birthday on Facebook, they respond by saying,

"Hey, if you're ever hiring again, keep me in mind. That was the coolest place I ever worked, and I loved it." They still email me and show me various awards they've won, even though I haven't been with the company in twelve years. Some have told me they still keep work anniversary photos and cards with my handwritten messages on their desks, because their time at Platinum was fun and filled with great memories.

STAND APART

It's a hard fact that another company can come in and steal your employees, or present them with a great new job offer. To prevent this from happening, there has to be a differentiation between your company and the one across the street—you have to stand apart so your employees don't accept that offer.

At Platinum, we did our best to stand apart from the competition. Every first Friday of the month, we got everyone in the company together to share results and communicate how we were doing. We'd share good news, bad news, and then have time for Q&A. This helped our 275 employees understand and appreciate where we stood as a company, and as a team. We also had an option program for key management so they felt invested in the success of the business, personally and professionally.

At CEO Coaching International, we're very inclusive and mindful of our partners. My wife and I get together with leaders and their spouses as often as we can because it's fun, and we believe it builds a good culture. Last year, we took everyone from our leadership team to Cabo, along with their spouses. This year, we're taking our Executive Leadership Team to a home in Tuscany. These trips encourage spouses to be included in the journey and what we stand for.

LIKE TO LOVE

Quality leadership is a must if you want to move people from like to love, but you must hire passionate people from the start—you don't want to hire misfits or prima donnas. Employees have to believe in what you stand for, and live and share your values. They must work at your company for the right reasons, and you have to get the right people into the right roles.

ROBERT GLAZER, CEO OF ACCELERATION PARTNERS

Robert Glazer is an entrepreneur, author, speaker, and founder and CEO of Acceleration Partners, a global performance marketing agency. He believes in inspiring people and encouraging them to do more in all areas of their lives, and he openly demonstrates this in the way he runs this company. Employees obviously love the company, because it has a rating of 4.9 on Glassdoor and was named the fourth best place to work in 2018 by Glassdoor's Small-to-Medium-Sized Business Employee Choice Awards. The company has also experienced a 40 percent increase in business and a lower rate of turnover after implementing unique, breakthrough practices.

A FOCUS ON CULTURE

Many companies put pressure on employees by setting massive goals that require them to put work above everything else. Attaining these goals may help the company become profitable and appear to be successful in the public eye, but within its walls there will be resentful, tired, and uninspired employees. This is exactly what I want to avoid. Success can't come at the cost of employee happiness—that will never move them from like to love.

I would rather win culture awards, instead of ones that highlight growth, products, or service. While those awards are excellent and make companies proud, culture is the key to attracting the brightest and best employees. You need innovative brand advocates that can help the company reach the next level.

At Acceleration Partners, we avoid a negative practice that was mentioned earlier in this book: clinging to the past. We have a healthy respect for tradition and appreciate what has made us successful, but we don't rely on it to propel us forward. We are constantly evolving, which means we are aware of the need to change roles and processes. As difficult as it may be to part ways with someone who was essential in the early days of our growth, we are able to recognize if and when that person doesn't reflect our new vision, or if they no longer help to move the company forward.

ACCELERATION PARTNERS (AP) SUMMIT

The AP Summit is an annual event for *all* employees, not just leadership. It highlights our company vision, goals, and accomplishments. Team members give presentations in the style of "TED Talks," and they aren't limited to company topics. Someone might give a presentation about building strong business relationships, and the next one will be about time management for work and life, and the importance of establishing morning routines for happiness and productivity—we discuss anything that can affect performance and engagement at work.

The group also participates in community service activities, ranging from sending cards to people on active duty in the military to working in thrift stores and helping with Habitat for Humanity projects. We also have fun events like karaoke contests, and a field day with relays and various competitions.

A unique feature of the AP Summit is the "Core Value Awards" dinner. This is similar to many award ceremonies that celebrate high performers and successes, but we also take the time to highlight employees who consistently demonstrate our values. We even give an award for "Rookie of the Year."

At the ten-year anniversary Summit, I asked employees to list their "top five" life goals and dreams. Then, I chose ten reoccurring themes from the collective of goals and surprised employees by helping to make their dreams come true. I hired my personal trainer to help some train for marathons and triathlons, hired a book publishing company to coach others on how to write a book, purchased guitar lessons for another, and sent another to flight school. These are just a few of the things I did. I know this sounds extravagant, and it may not be realistic for your company, team, or budget, but asking employees about their goals outside of work gives you an idea of how to best support them, and help make their dreams come true.

MINDFUL TRANSITIONS

We've eliminated the traditional expectation and practice of giving a two-week notice when leaving a job. We call this an "open transition," and it eliminates the downhill slope of disengagement as an employee begins searching and interviewing for new jobs. It also helps prevent resentful or surprised management and coworkers after notice has been given; they often have to pick up the slack and rush to find a replacement. Open transitions allow the time to slowly transfer responsibilities, rather than suddenly dump them on others. This greatly benefits the person leaving, their boss, and their coworkers. In this seamless transition, many stressors can be avoided and the manager can focus on business without distractions.

In my third book, *Mindful Transitions*, I'm writing about the company's unique program to create a safe environment where employees can share their plans for the future, even if their plan is to leave company. This leads to mutual trust, frequent communication, and a happy, healthy workforce. These mindful transitions work because we reaffirm the company's core values on a regular basis, and I meet with employees frequently. I believe regular feedback is essential—you can't wait until an end-of-year review to find out an employee has been struggling. By having regular meetings, both employer and employee know where they stand, and they can work together to come up with creative solutions. For example, the employer can offer to change employee responsibilities within their current role, or find a new role within the company that is a better fit.

CAPACITY BUILDING

I send a newsletter to employees every Friday, and this eventually evolved into the "Friday Forward" (www.fridayfwd.com). The blog now has 35,000 followers around the world; many are leaders who share its inspirational messages with their teams. These messages have evolved, and I'm currently writing a book called: *Outperform: Unlocking and Building Capacity in Yourself and Others*, where I share my philosophy on how to grow and develop employees, and how to best impact your business. I'll conclude this section with thoughts on capacity building:

> We need to find ways to outperform ourselves and our own expectations. We need to continuously build our capacity both individually, and collectively.

> Inspiration is important and is often the catalyst for growth, but just wanting to be better is never enough. What I have discovered is that the ability to outperform—to exceed expectations—is directly related to the ability to build capacity in yourself and others. Capacity building is similar to a muscle: it's something that needs to be built up over time and doesn't happen overnight. For example, I may be inspired to lift a heavy weight, but only after weeks of incremental improvement will I have built up the strength and physical ability to do so. I've discovered that people's ability to do more in life works in very much the same way.

This discovery has led to a different way of thinking about people in our business. Today, we invest as much time as we do resources into training our employees holistically. We want them to achieve more across all areas of their life (work-life integration), as well as develop job-related skills. In doing so, not only are they happier and more fulfilled— they are also better equipped to meet the challenges and needs of our business as it grows. It's the ultimate win-win.

DAVID STILLMAN, GENERATIONS EXPERT

A healthy company culture and the war for talent are just two of the many concerns we address in the workplace today. We want engaged employees but in order to achieve this, we must recognize the changing needs and expectations of the younger generation, and how they differ from the older ones. We can't do things the way we've always done them. These words from David Stillman, best-selling author of *When Generations Collide: Who They Are. Why They Clash. How to Solve the Generational Puzzle at Work*, *The M Factor: How the Millennial Generation Is Rocking the Workplace*, and *Gen Z at Work: How the Next Generation Is Transforming the Workplace*, are just a drop in the ocean, but hopefully give you a starting point to navigate the generational gap.

In the past, leadership never asked employees what would make them happy in their jobs. The question in itself is Millennial-centric. The general view of employers was that people were lucky to have their jobs, and there weren't any needs to be met. Older generations may be resentful of employers because no one ever asked them what *they* wanted.

Older generations tend to see the younger ones as entitled or self-centered because they ask for what they want and need in their jobs. However, what is often characterized as entitlement is really *expectation*. It's important to realize that they do this because of how they were raised. The parents of Millennials, in particular, taught them that their voices matter, and they need to speak up. For this reason, they begin their jobs with the expectation that others will listen to what they have to say.

Millennials are collaborative, and they like to think in groups and tribes. This generation will move from like to love if they can view their peers at work as family; their teammates are important to them. Advancement opportunities are also key because they had the rug pulled out from under them in the recent recession, they have mounds of college debt, and may even feel a little threatened by Gen Z coming through the door. They want to move up the ladder, and need to believe their company is truly investing in them.

Millennials need the freedom to express themselves in the workplace, but they must also be passionate about their jobs—they must have meaning. If they're going to work somewhere for eight to ten hours per day, or dedicate their lives to a career, it has to be significant and make a difference somehow, somewhere. This generation is happy when they know that what they do contributes to a greater good.

GEN Z

It's important to make a distinction between Gen Z and Millennials; they aren't of the same generation. Gen Z had a completely different upbringing, so meaning and passion won't interest them. They came of age during the recent recession, and their parents didn't tell them they could be anything they wanted to be. This generation is in survival mode. While meaning and impact can still be a factor in Gen Z job selection, you must offer good pay to even get them through the door. If your salary is not competitive, or better, they will not come work for you. Period.

So, what will get a Gen Z from like to love? How do you make sure they don't leave for another organization that also offers competitive pay and salary? Your culture must address their FOMO, or fear of missing out. You must provide education, training, and advancement opportunities that create the notion that they'll be missing out if they go elsewhere. This generation likes to wear lots of different hats, and does not want to be in one position or career forever. If they are able to do a variety of things, they will love their job and the organization, and they'll know they aren't missing out.

CULTURE

Culture is a high priority for every company, and each generation has a different idea about what an engaging culture looks like. To get this right, instead of asking *how* is our culture, companies need to ask, *what* is our culture? For example, Gen Z may not care that the office walls are painted beautifully, or that there are inspirational messages posted throughout the building. This generation prefers to work screen-to-screen, and company cultures need to evolve to accommodate changing expectations.

WORK-LIFE BLEND

For years, we've been chasing work-life balance, and it's still an ongoing battle. In the past, if we worked too hard, it was time to dial it back. Or if we weren't working enough, we needed to work more, or work harder. Older generations have yet to conquer work-life balance and I doubt we ever will, but I believe Gen Z has a good handle on it. What we call work-life integration, they call *work-life blend*.

This concept embraces the fact that work and life are both 24/7, and this changes where, when, and how we work. For instance, if I have an appointment from noon to two, it doesn't affect my work because I log that time from eight to ten at night. Or, if I need to be gone all day Thursday, I don't consider that a vacation day because I can come in on Saturday and get caught up. Work-life blend no longer views work as what happens from nine to five, Monday through Friday, and life being what happens during the other hours—work and life are truly blended.

Side Hustles

Nowadays, it seems like everyone has a "side hustle," or a way to make supplemental income. The younger the group, the more side hustles there are. Seventy-five percent of Gen Z have a side hustle, and plan to continue them for their entire lives. This can present a challenge in workplaces today.

People used to go to work, and then they'd work on their side hustle at home. With work-life blend, employees might work on their side hustle during the day; you might walk by someone's desk and see them uploading pictures to a website where they are selling goods. If an employer is angered by that, the employee might counter by saying, "Well, you email me at 8:00 p.m., and I always respond." If we truly believe in work-life blend, and employees are expected to bring work into their life, they should be allowed to bring life into their work.

EMBRACE REALITY

You must be realistic in your job descriptions and expectations of employees from the very beginning, or else you will find people throughout your company who do *not* love their jobs. If showing up at 7:00 a.m. to answer the phones is part of the job, you must communicate that during the recruiting process so an employee knows what they're signing up for. If they accept those terms, they are more likely to fall in love with their job. However, if you paint a picture that makes the job seem rosier than it truly is, employees can become resentful. As an employer, it may be tempting to talk about what you want or believe you can offer, when it's quite possible that you can't. By being transparent and embracing reality, it will get your people to love much quicker.

WAR FOR TALENT

The war for talent has many companies scrambling to get young people through the door—ample time, money, and effort are spent to recruit and retain them. Companies believe it will be a detriment if they lose this age group. It's fine for employers to focus on Millennials and Gen Z, but they have to show love to the Boomers and Xers, too. When we think of training and development, we typically think of the needs of new hires: onboarding and preparing them for their jobs. We don't think of the loyal fifty-five-year-old employee who is dying to learn. Can you remember the last time you sent an existing employee to a training course?

We asked Baby Boomers across the country what makes them stay at their jobs. The number one answer was, "Making an impact." They don't like to go to work and constantly hear about the younger generation, or listen to their bosses complain about all the company is unable to do. They will leave because they won't love their job, and no one is paying attention to them.

Older generations want to leave a legacy—they're definitely not ready to leave yet. Make sure you aren't falling into an "out with the old, in with the new" mindset. Love is a lot easier to generate with these age groups than you think, and you might even create more value with them.

We tend to think we're in a safe place with the older generation, and will have no problem retaining them—we think they're fully coached, and they have all they need. Many companies assume love is forever with them, but the truth is, someone else can come along and dazzle them. We're seeing nonprofits scoop up Boomers by offering them an opportunity to leave a legacy.

LIKE TO LOVE

Companies should take responsibility for moving their employees from like to love, but they must keep in mind that employees control half of the equation. Like to love isn't just about salaries, flexible schedules, or nailing the work-life blend. When people love their jobs, there's a good chance they're also happy in their lives. People who are generally miserable often bring their misery into the workplace—a great performer can still be a downer who negatively affects your culture. It's quite possible you've done everything right, but some people are just unhappy no matter what. You can do your best to make positive contributions to your culture when you hire: look for happy people who have the potential to love their jobs.

CONCLUSION

Getting your customers from like to love is critical to the success of your organization, and the number one way to do it is by getting your *employees* from like to love.

If your employees love their jobs, they will deliver exceptional service inside and outside the organization. They become brand advocates and they love working with their team.

Once you have a base of employees who love the company, apply what you learn from them and begin to create a company-wide change of perspective. It's critical to get your employees to love their jobs so they can help you build customer loyalty to your brand.

If an employee doesn't love being at your company, it can be problematic. This person will eventually cause damage. Their negativity will affect other team members, hurt customer relationships, and hurt your bottom line. Fortunately, there are a number of simple and highly effective ways to meet every employee's five basic needs. Remember, they want care, trust, listening and clear communication, empowerment and recognition, and a meaningful purpose. Give them those things, and they will love what they do.

What can you do today to transition everyone in your business from like to love? My hope is that this book has inspired you and provided you with the process and tools to begin this journey.

In everything you do, think about your end goal: moving people from like to love.

I hope you've learned from this book, and I'd love the opportunity to have a discussion with you. The Nitrous Effect can help you begin making the transition from like to love and see incredible changes in employee engagement. To learn more, please contact us at:

The Nitrous Effect
www.NitrousEffect.com
314.367.2255

LIKE TO LOVE REFERENCE PAGE

The five basic needs are:

1. You Genuinely Care about Me
2. I Trust You and You Trust Me
3. You Listen to Me
4. You Appreciate Me for Who I Am and You Tell Me So
5. We Share a Meaningful Purpose

For more information and bonus material:
www.fromliketo.love

For information on the Nitrous Effect Agencies:
www.NitrousEffect.com

To contact the author: www.KeithAlper.com

ABOUT THE AUTHOR

KEITH ALPER has loved every job he's ever had. The love never came from compensation—it was because of company cultures and the people he worked with. With the belief that everyone should love their organization and the goal of spreading the gospel of employee engagement, he founded CPG Agency over thirty years ago, at the age of eighteen.

Since then, CPG has expanded into a seven-agency collective known as The Nitrous Effect. The agency specializes in branding, marketing, and corporate culture and engagement events, with a strong focus on innovation and entrepreneurship. The Nitrous Effect serves many Fortune

500 clients, including Southwest Airlines, Carnival Cruise Line, Boeing, Bridgestone, and Virgin Hotels.

Keith is an expert in entertainment, digital media, and marketing. He has produced special events, meetings, videos, films, broadcasts, and major entertainment projects around the world. He has been featured in *The Wall Street Journal*, *The New York Times*, *Inc.*, and *Fortune* magazine. In addition to receiving over two hundred industry awards, he is a recipient of the Inc. 500 Top 100 Multimedia Producers award, and has been on the Event Marketer It List.